Between the Sheets

An Intimate Exchange
About Writing, Editing,
and Publishing

By Thomas T. Thomas
and
Kate Campbell

BETWEEN THE SHEETS:
An Intimate Exchange About Writing,
Editing, and Publishing

Cover photo © 2011 Simon Bond

ISBN: 978-1-4751209-3-6

Contents

"Grammar is a piano I play by ear.
All I know about grammar is its power."

—Joan Didion

This discussion about writing, editing,
and publishing is dedicated to those
who love the alchemy of words
and the magic of stories.

Introduction

"A book is like a man—clever and dull, brave and cowardly, beautiful and ugly," novelist John Steinbeck wrote. "For every flowering thought there will be a page like a wet and mangy mongrel." The Nobel Laureate made this observation to his long-time editor and friend Pascal (Pat) Covici. It was included in what Steinbeck envisioned as the prologue to his 1952 novel *East of Eden,* which is dedicated to Covici.

"Well—then the book is done," Steinbeck told Covici. "It has no virtue any more. The writer wants to cry out—'Bring it back! Let me rewrite it or better—Let me burn it. Don't let it out in the unfriendly cold in that condition.' " Ultimately, the original prologue was dropped in the editing process, but it is included in the posthumously published *Journal of a Novel,* a collection of letters to Covici written during the creation of *East of Eden.* Steinbeck, who wrote in longhand, began each day's writing with a letter to Pat. When the novel was finished, the letters were sent to Covici, along with the original manuscript, in a hand-carved mahogany chest Steinbeck built for the purpose.

Having just completed my first novel and gone through the final editing process with my long-time friend and editor, the novelist Tom Thomas, I have a sense of what Steinbeck was feeling when he turned the manuscript over to what he called the "lions"—editors, designers, publishers, marketing experts, and critics. Although I was ready to let go of the project, I didn't want to send my darling out in public in a homemade dress and scuffed shoes. I wanted it to be my best work, dressed for success, star of the grammar school spelling bee.

Tom graciously agreed to take on the editing project, and during an intense four-month period, we worked on the final editing of *Adrift in the Sound.* In the process, through more than 70 email exchanges, Tom schooled me in the thinking of literary editors and the fine points of writing, as well as analysis of current publishing trends and marketing techniques. The email exchange is instructive and lavish, more than I deserve, really. I kept the correspondence to reread for its valuable content. Email is ephemeral, just hit delete and the messages disappear. I didn't want that to happen with Tom's messages and it had occurred to me early in our exchanges that Tom's letters were extraordinary and should be shared with other writers, teachers and literary scholars—really anyone interested in peeking behind the curtain to see what goes on between writer and editor in the final throes of shaping a book for readers.

I wrote *Adrift in the Sound* for many reasons: to please myself, to experiment, to prove I can work in long-form fiction, to show off, to escape, to share the experience of an era with my children, to capture a piece of modern history, to create an enduring work of art. Tom, pragmatic and clear-eyed, edited the book with a commitment to having the story serve the needs of the reader. In Steinbeck's aborted prologue to *East of Eden*, he wrote: "There you are Pat. You came in with a box of glory and there you stand with an armful of damp garbage. And … a new character has emerged. He is called the Reader."

The Reader
He is so stupid you can't trust him with an idea.
He is so clever he will catch you in the least error.
He will not buy short books.
He will not buy long books.
He is part moron, part genius and part ogre.
There is some doubt as to whether he can read.

Although Steinbeck's view of The Reader is clearly in jest, you'll see Tom never kidded around about the honor readers pay an author with their time and attention. His work on *Adrift* aimed at serving the reader's needs for fullness, flow, and accuracy in storytelling, among many other things. My goal for the story was to beguile the reader, delight him or her, breathe life into a world of my own creation, dignify my characters, put my experience into a form that can be widely understood, and leave the reader pondering what had taken place in the story, in the world, long after it ends. Tom's values and my intentions are enfolded in the final version of the book.

Many years ago, when I was in journalism school at San Francisco State University, my professor, an acclaimed newspaper editor and reporter, told me: "Love your editors. You're gonna need 'em." I took the advice to heart.

— Kate Campbell

From: Kate
Sent: Wednesday, August 10, 2011, 7:31 PM
Subject: Adrift in the Sound

Dear Elizabeth[1] & Tom:

In preparation for our meeting Sept. 3, I've been trying to find a good, reasonably priced copy editor to prepare *Adrift in the Sound* for publishing. I found a couple online and emailed them a copy of the manuscript. My son read their responses and says they're playing me with the "engaging voice" comment, and how my project would be a good fit for their expertise, setting me up to take on more needless debt by preying on my hopes and clamping on my credit card. My son says it's doubtful these guys did more than read a few passages from the manuscript just so they'd have something to say.

I've already gotten a quote of $1,500 from one of novelist Stephen King's early editors. He's telling me I must trust him completely like some oily Svengali and that his services are constantly in demand, and there is currently a waiting list for his help. He warns that a delay of several weeks is possible before he can begin an edit, but the money up-front will earn me a place in line.

He says his approach is not to help me write prettier sentences, but to closely evaluate my manuscript from a publisher's perspective and identify and remove every issue that could lead to rejection. Then, he says, I'll be ready for a thorough rewrite prior to publisher submission, which he says, if I follow his direction, should improve my chances of success. He's interested in shaping commercial fiction, not literary fiction, which I gather he thinks is the purview of English teachers who focus on the literary classics and don't know what they're doing in the commercial sense.

The second editor looked at the manuscript sent by email and wrote: "Hi Kate ~ *Adrift in the Sound* is very well written—*intelligently* written—but it would definitely benefit from a professional edit, mainly to fix dialogue paragraphing (sometimes it's hard to figure out who's speaking), to tweak comma placement and some other punctuation to improve sentence clarity, and to firm up viewpoint here and there. Mostly, it needs a *careful* edit. Your narrative voice is very engaging.

The last thing you want is a heavy-handed edit that would interfere with that voice."

The second editor is right about one thing. I don't want a heavy-handed edit designed to generate mass-market pulp, one that interferes or destroys the novel's authorial voice and lyricism. I want help with dialog tags, point of view shifts, yes, and I want to get the commas cleaned up. But, I can't and won't pay $3,500 for this service. I'm not sure I'd pay $1,500 to somebody who promises to use a meat ax on the manuscript to trigger a massive rewrite, not after four years and dozens of rewrites and endless polishing. I'm afraid these guys are Charlatans preying on those desperate to be published.

I've tried to create a work of art, not commercial fiction. I publish everyday and don't lust to see my name in print. Any ideas about where else to look for a deft, affordable copy editor? Tom, I hate to ask, but would you have time to look at a small piece of the manuscript to see how bad it is and how much help you think is needed? Elizabeth has already read the entire book in earlier drafts. (Thanks for that.) Any advice you can offer on how to get the manuscript up to snuff is most appreciated.

Notes:

1. Elizabeth Kern (http://elizabethkern.com/), a mutual friend, Kate's writing partner, and a former colleague, also writes fiction. Her debut novel is *Wanting to Be Jackie Kennedy.*

From: Tom
Sent: Thursday, August 11, 2011, 10:48 AM
Subject: Re: Adrift in the Sound

Kate—

The digital self-publishing world is still in transition. One day—probably in a year or two, based on how fast things are going—there will be on-line resource markets where editors, cover illustrators, and HTML coders can offer their services with some uniformity of description and a reasonable pricing structure. That's what you're looking for. In the meantime, I think of the editing job in two ways: copy editing and structural editing.

Copy editors work with things that are obviously wrong in terms of standard English: punctuation, typos, word usage, awkward sentences, continuity ("this shirt was a sweater on page 98") and other obvious errors. A copy editor would also offer observations about confusion as to who's speaking the dialog, but change it only if the fix was obvious (add "Jane said" here and "Clyde said" there). But if the book is going off the track, like not showing how or why they got to Rome after dining in Paris, or whole passages of dialog are banal and obvious and don't move the reader forward, or the ending is really no good—then you need something stronger.

Structural editors look at the book as an artistic whole. This is what a book acquisitions editor does, generally working with an author whose book he or she or the house has already decided has a potential market and should be published. The structural editor works with the author, rather than taking the manuscript in hand and fixing things him/herself automatically, like a copy editor.

For example: "You tell us Jane's a kleptomaniac and has no control over her urges, but it would be helpful if you actually showed her in the act and examined her feelings through internal dialog." Or, "We already know Jane's a kleptomaniac, so the fourth trip to the store starting on page 57 is really unnecessary." "I find the character of Benjamin inconsistent: he says nasty things at the party, but we don't know why. Then everyone says what a good guy he is. We need some insight here." "Your ending would be stronger if, instead of Carmen just walking away when Camille kills the dog, Carmen took some action that the reader can identify with." The structural editor will suggest improvements in line with your original or perceived intentions, but he/she won't rewrite the book for you. (That's why advances make a distinction between "on signing" and "on delivery of an acceptable manuscript.")

Right now, we're still in the mode where a freelance editor thinks he's helping you get your book ready for a publisher's view. You're right to be suspicious, because the decision to publish has not traditionally been based on a few typos or dialog changes or even some structural flaws. The publisher looks at the market: "Can I sell this? Is the topic going to attract the readers Xanadu House serves? What marketing hooks are available in the story to help me promote this book?"

A perfectly written manuscript that has no market potential won't get published by a traditional paper publisher, who has to put tens of thousands of dollars into editing, typesetting, cover, press run, distribution, etc. before it can find its first reader. A sloppy manuscript with lots of careless errors and odious dialog might put off an editor before he or she gets far enough into the story to establish marketability or its lack, but perfection of the whole structure and every sentence is not a prerequisite for attracting a publisher. (Of course, under today's cost pressures, the traditional publishers are willing to spend less time trying to make a book right, so a well edited book has a better chance—provided it fits the market in the first place.)

In any case, no first-time author, not even an established author unless he has a bestseller track record, will be showing the new work directly to an acquisitions editor. Sending a book to a publisher ("throwing it over the transom") only lands it on the slush pile. As an editor I read tons of slush. You quickly identify authors who in desperation have sent their books to the wrong house (novels to an academic publisher, say) and those who for all the paper in the world can't get to what they have to say. They get polite "not for us" replies.

Once in a hundred manuscripts you get a book that is almost on target and with a little structural work could be really quite good. The editor would like to take the author in hand and offer these suggestions, but then the senior editor wisely asks, "Say you did all that rewriting, would you publish the book?" "Well, no, but it would be a better book." "Then send them a polite 'not for us' reply." Reading slush is like looking for diamonds in a pigsty—not hopeless, but heartbreaking.

So traditional publishing depends on author's agents as their intake channel. Today the hurdle for a writer is finding an agent, not a publisher. You approach an agent in the same way you do a publisher. And once you land an agent, he or she may put you in touch with a structural or copy editor, so the book looks better when he/she presents it to a publisher for consideration. But the agent is going to look at the same things as a publisher: marketability. (An agent also wants to know how likely you are to write a second, third ... tenth book. One-off masterpieces are not for them.)

Uniqueness has its benefits, but being so unique that it falls outside any genre or market is a bad thing. (Really unique books sometimes—million-to-one, lottery odds—get routine turndowns until they find a niche publisher: J. K. Rowling finally landed with Scholastic; Tom Clancy was picked up at Naval Institute Press.) Most agents will try a book with three mainstream publishers, and if it doesn't fly by then, tell you to go back and write a different book. Most agents today have so many authors they can't sell that they won't take you on in the first place.

In this market, most freelance editors are bottom feeders playing on the hopes of desperate unpublished authors. They'll take your money and never, good heavens, guarantee that the book will be publishable. Most vanity presses are also down in the mud. They'll print 3,000 copies of your book and wish you well in selling them out of your garage.

Some, like Smashwords, are getting into digital and POD (print-on-demand) publishing, but you need to examine their service package closely.[1] Digital self-publishing is changing all that, because there's no paper book to hold and distribute. But you still need to market yourself—and there are bottom feeders there, too. But traditional publishers today do very little marketing—authors are expected to get themselves to conventions and book fairs and public readings on their own, print and distribute postcards of their book cover, etc.

So that's the background. To your questions:

(1) The second editor has probably read more than a few passages, but no one is going to read the whole book before telling you they'll edit it. But $3,500 sounds high for copy editing—unless you've written *Moby Dick*.

(2) The first editor sounds like he's trading on the King name. (My last agent was Kirby McCauley, who was Stephen King's first agent and was supposed to be able to "call down the lightning.") It sounds like he's going to do structural editing, and $1,500 sounds low for that. And yes, a contractor who insists you "trust him completely" sounds suspicious. The money-equals-place-in-line ploy also sounds suspicious. Consider, finally, that King's first book was around 1970 (he

and I are of an age), so if the guy was established when King was not, he's got to be at least in his 70s by now. Not saying that makes him a bad editor, but what has he done for the literary world in 41 years? Any other names you'd know?

(3) If you've written art rather than commercial fiction ... why are you looking for an editor? Bind the manuscript with pink ribbon and put it on the shelf. It's an artwork. You look for an editor because you want someone else to read it, and that's *commerce,* baby! The wonderful thing about epublishing is that it blows all the genres apart. Genres are the way publishers categorize their market: science fiction, fantasy, sword & sorcery, *Star Trek* tie-in, D&D tie-in ... romance, historical romance, glitz[2] ... detective, true crime, police procedural ... these markets multiply faster than a nest of mice. But the new combination of easy publishing (Kindle/Nook/iBooks) and easy marketing (internet pages and social media) means you can hope to reach just the thousand or so readers who aren't looking for "police procedural" or "glitz" but the particular type of story and view that Kate Campbell writes. You're a market of one. You build it by word of mouth.

(4) Yes, I'll read *Adrift in the Sound.* Send me the first couple of chapters and a brief outline (page or so) of what happens from there. If I get it soon, I'll read before we meet on September 3.

Notes:

1. I've heard authors on the LinkedIn Writer's Network complain that their POD publisher put the price of the book so high—e.g., $34.95 for a children's book—that they will never make a sale.

2. Glitz—go look it up; it's in *The Literary Marketplace.* Glitz is the sort of romance novel Danielle Steel writes, or that got on television as "Dallas." The life and loves of a young woman who's heir to a fortune so grand that her life choices are buying another yacht or invading a small country. Yeah, there's a market for that kind of book. GAH!

From: Kate
Sent: Thursday, August 11, 2011, 3:08 PM
Subject: Re: Adrift in the Sound

And, where is this erudite wisdom of yours on the role of editors in an imploding publishing world going to be printed? It is the best, clearest explanation about how today's writing and publishing world works that I've ever read. I cannot stand for you to waste this insightful analysis on me. It has to be shared somehow. That's my way of saying thanks, by paying it forward to others who will benefit from reviewing your perspective. Your Web site, my blog, an essay for *Writer's Digest*? Where can it be published? Really good stuff. Damn!

From: Tom
Sent: Thursday, August 11, 2011, 4:53 PM
Subject: Fish to Fry

Thanks, Kate. I'm collecting these responses I've been making about writing—to you, elsewhere to the Writer's Network—and will package them as a series on my blog (http://www.thomastthomas.com/Art_Blogs.htm). But, for now, I've got other fish to fry. It's a good idea in blogging to hold off on something you already have in mind until the well goes dry. Like writing a column for the newspaper, you always want to have a couple of items "on the hook."

From: Kate
Sent: Thursday, August 11, 2011, 7:02 PM
Subject: Taking a Look

Hi Tom:

I know you're busy and appreciate you finding time to take a look at the opening to *Adrift in the Sound,* a 92,000-word mainstream literary novel. I've attached the first 25 pages and a story summary.

From: Tom
Sent: Thursday, August 18, 2011, 10:50 AM
Subject: Critical Read

First, I want to thank you for the offer of letting me read the first chapters of *Adrift in the Sound.* It's an interesting book and has the potential, I think, to explain a time and a mindset that affected all of us Boomers. It's certainly a book I could not write.

I've spent a certain amount of time with this, read the text closely, and offered perhaps more comments than you want to see. Nothing I found here is a story killer—although I think you're going to have to rethink and rewrite the whale-collision scene, for the reasons I give. But my intention was not to read as your friend and then praise your book.

Take as a given that if I don't mark something, it's good stuff. As an old book editor, I read critically, adopting the pose of a knowledgeable lay reader who's just bought your book and wants to know what's going on. So if I mark something, it's where I stumbled or grumbled or came up short. Think of my role in editor mode as being your "eyes behind," watching the author's back and catching the things she might not see for herself, being so close to the work.

As to whether you need a structural editor or just a copy editor … I found you need very little copy editing and what needs to be done there would fly like a pencil across the page. The structural items aren't major, but they involve word choices, the pictures you're painting as you go along, and some basic questions such as, is Lizette a slacker, troubled but with artistic aspiration, or mentally ill? Is Rocket a smart guy or a doofus? Those things a structural editor can point out, but only you can decide and then fix. I wouldn't engage anyone to work on the text until you let it go really cold in your head, come back and read with "fresh eyes," and do what I call a "snowplow" edit on yourself that clears away the excess and makes the strong points stand out.

Don't be discouraged. I think this book has real potential. We can talk over some of these points on the 3rd.

[Attachment follows]

Tom Thomas Cover Notes

There's some good stuff here, and it's an intriguing notion to tell about "the day the music died" in terms of the hopeful Sixties turning into the dreadful Seventies. I like that you've picked a frame character like Lizette, apparently dull and damaged from the viewpoint of everyone around her, but really seeing more than she lets on and stronger than she looks.

I've read through your chapters with "track changes" turned on and made copious comments. This is a mixed editing job. You need very little copy editing of the period-and-comma sort. But you need to do a certain amount of self-editing and some modest rewrites for issues that an outside reader can raise and suggest, but only you can resolve.

You'll find a lot of comments here, and most of them will seem awfully picky, weighing word choices and meanings and the backgrounds of things. Anymore, when I read fiction, I tend to be very linear—as most readers are. We're all getting the story one word, one sentence, one thought and image at a time. If there's a tangent or something improbable, I tend to look back and compare it with what is already known, rather than leaping ahead to see what is yet to be revealed. If I have a suspicion or a question, I'll only carry it so far—usually just a sentence or so. If I have to carry it too far, page after page, that's a clue to me that the author is creating a mystery, but then the answer to my question had better be big and satisfying, not some piddling detail I could easily have been given in proper order.

In genre fiction, like science fiction or the sort of spy thriller/action books that Pat Larkin[1] writes, the reader can take a lot for granted about the characters' emotions and motives. The hero's or heroine's feelings and intentions are a given, and description goes into the kind of weapon being used and how the ambush was set up. Most of the details are known or dropped in passing to provide color or assist in developing a political mystery, and let's get on with the action! But in literary fiction—especially where the author is building a feeling for time and place and character purely out of word choices, and the meaning of everything is not clear—then the reader is more of a detective, weighing words as clues to the emotional context.

The complexity of this is doubled or tripled when we begin to suspect (from clues like "When did you get out?" and "welfare checks" and the "lumpy bag") that Lizette is a special case and perhaps even mentally ill. And we suspect that Einar (from his fumbling and emaciation) is either emotionally dense or, as Lizette suspects, senile. In this sort of complexity, with the reader playing detective to learn what is going on—because like a good author you're showing us, rather than telling us—the little details do matter.

So, in my reading and commenting, I'm trying to give you an appreciation of what the reader is experiencing as he/she comes upon the "found object" that is your story.

1. Let the Story Go Cold, Then Edit Yourself

One of the most valuable things I've learned as a writer—and I can't always do it consistently myself—is to be a good forgetter. When I'm done writing a passage, I try to let it go cold, dissipate, vanish. This takes a few days. Then, when I return to it, read word for word, as if for the first time. That's the way to find the traps of "How do I (the reader) know this if I (the author) haven't explained it yet?" Linear in words is also linear in time, and the editor's job—and the author's job as a rewriter—is to put details in correct order so that all is revealed, all questions in the reader's mind satisfied—or raised as mysteries to be hungrily anticipated. It helps to hold multiple personalities while you're doing this. "I actually know what happens next but I'm pretending I don't."

2. Words Paint Pictures and Take the Readers in Certain Directions

The reader will try to catch every ball you toss. Unlike the pitcher on the mound, however, you have to toss most balls so they're easy to catch. If you throw a curve, it must be intentional, designed to trap or tease the reader with a mystery. Never send the reader diving for an image you didn't intend in the first place.

Some examples … On page 4,[2] Lizette watches her father's shoulders as he makes tea. You use the word "muscles." Men's muscles don't normally show under a plaid shirt, which is usually thick and made of flannel or wool. So I got the impression of a muscular man. But two sentences later you describe him as having a "clothes-hanger frame" and his shirt gathered at the belt. That gave me a moment of disjunction that distracts from the reading.

On page 8, he offers Lizette art supplies from the studio and makes a point of that place being, for him, like an abandoned village. But then she says she'll take a palette knife and starts looking around the kitchen for it. The reader's thoughts are out in the studio, dwelling on its sadness. This inspection of the kitchen creates disjunction.

On page 13, you describe guys going into "the Dog House" next to Sandy's. I immediately thought this was a bar or restaurant. (I even corrected later use of "the Dogs' house" under this impression.) It's not until the middle of the next chapter that we learn the Dogs are a softball team who hang out in Rocket's or Bomber's or Sandy's half-abandoned house. A little more description of the street and who these people are, coming up front on page 4, would not hurt the flow and would make the setting of casual squatting there easier for the reader to understand.

Because readers are reading closely to understand the world you're showing, we also pay attention to "stage business." We never know whether a sled named "Rosebud" might be an artless toss-off or something important. Among other things going on in Chapter 3, Rocket starts boiling three eggs. Then he takes them off the stove and burns his fingers. Then—as far as I can tell on a careful reading—they disappear from the story entirely. Not eaten or thrown out. I worry about those eggs!

On page 22, Rocket retires to his bunk with a children's book about whales. We've already seen from the previous chapter that he's smarter than the hopeless Bomber, that Rocket's the founder and mainstay of this Dogs' house group, and that he treasures and even can play a fine vintage piano. But in the bunk he comes across as a simpleton: reading with his finger, amazed at factoids he's read before. This is suddenly the Lenny from (John Steinbeck's) *Of Mice and Men*. Since we've gathered that Rocket is going to be an important character, the disjunction is disturbing. If it's intentional (he's actually the best of a band of really stupid brothers) then it needs to be explained more directly. On the deck of the tugboat, especially during the crisis, Rocket is also shown to be a fuckup: causing the boat to leave late, throwing the wrong lines in securing the injured whale, knocking a man overboard in tossing a line. Is all that intentional? That is, is Rocket really stupid and useless? Or have you lost control of the story here while spinning your yarn?

On page 24, the tugboat is lifted "out of a wave trough," causing an emergency for all hands. As I explain in my note about the sudden appearance of the wounded orca, the boat is many times larger than the whale, and even a solid bump wouldn't lift the boat. (Look at some of the tugboats at Western Tow Boat [http://www.westerntowboat.com/Tugs/default.aspx] in Seattle. These are large, heavy boats—the 70 footers are almost 100 gross tons—with huge propellers to generate a lot of thrust for the work they do. Maybe the little 38 footer at 20 tons might generate a bump going over the six-ton whale, but not enough to rise out of the water.) The fact that the propeller cut into the whale works even more against the lifting you describe: the impact energy would go into slicing up the animal rather than into lifting the boat. That sudden bump and lift you describe sets up the wrong image of what's going on—as a reader I'm thinking perhaps they hit a submerged seamount or wreck?—and this image stays in the reader's mind when the whale suddenly appears on the surface. (Correcting this may need some rethinking and even rewriting of the whale rescue sequence.)

As writers, we try to create tiny universes a person can literally hold in his or her hands. We can make the reader believe many interesting things, but they will still test what we tell them against their own sense of reality. (As I tested the tugboat scene against what I know of boats and ships.) If we break the spell with some detail the reader knows to be false, or with careless use of words and meanings, it can break the whole spell.

3. Dialogue Paragraphing

As I note in comments, it's standard technique to open a new paragraph whenever a new speaker talks. I've made several changes in the early text—though certainly not all—to show this. Trying to follow the spirit of this standard, rather than just the letter of it, in my own writing I start a new paragraph at the response of one character to something said or done by another. And so, on page 6, when Einar offers "Pfeffernusse,"

Lizette's response of drawing back from her reverie starts a new paragraph.

You can jump overboard with this, creating paragraphs of single words and grunts that are followed by paragraphs of simple shrugs and nods. But the idea is that dialog isn't just words but an exchange of communication: question and answer, challenge and response, statement and thoughtful reflection. The spirit of this is like a tennis match, and I try to start a new paragraph at the point the ball goes over the net. (With judicious additions of "he said" and "she said," this will address some of the "whose talking?" comment your potential editor made.)

4. Point of View (POV) Mechanics

At this point, we're leaving the world of what any reader experiences for the world of Tom Thomas's personal way of writing. I am personally a point-of-view Nazi. My writing style is actually more "first person told in third person" than third person narrative. That is, to the best of my ability, there is no "omniscient narrator." What the reader sees and experiences is from the viewpoint and through the eyes and other senses of the character we ride in with. If I go to a second character, it's always in the context of a new scene.

With this restriction on my work, I love to create multi-character books, where the reader may know and understand things—because he or she has been inside several different heads—that any one character may not know or guess. (Only once, in *The Mask of Loki,* did I change viewpoints during a single scene, and then the reader's perspective traveled on the tip of a knife, from a person who is dying to the person who assassinated him.)

In this style, a POV character might suppose or guess what another is thinking or intending, but such suppositions and guesses must be clearly indicated as such. The POV character might recall details from earlier action, or offer as reflection things the reader needs to know about the setting and past relationships, but only if he or she experienced or heard about them firsthand. The character can't know about the gun in someone else's pocket without first seeing a bulge in the cloth, or know who's standing behind the door without hearing a scuffle or a whisper. (I would never use a construction like "What Max did not know is that Caroline had already returned home" or "Fred would never guess there was a dragon on the other side of the door.")

This is a hard way to write, a self-imposed straitjacket. But it's also, for me, a compass needle that always points north. I have to plan my stories to accommodate point of view, sometimes taking the action apart to put it in several different but contemporaneous scenes. I have to constantly question the details I reveal to make sure they don't violate character knowledge. But POV adherence also gives me a built-in pattern for weaving webs and creating surprise. (It's a key element in the plot of *The Judge's Daughter* and plays well between the two narrators in *First Citizen*.) Such rules, like the lines of perspective in a painting, limit your art but also give it strength.

In the chapters of *Adrift* that I've read so far, you mostly adhere to POV. The first chapter is mostly from Lizette's POV: what we see and know about Einar is what she sees and thinks or recalls. But then, on page 8, Lizette's talk of mixing paints "reassured Einar." I thought she was intentionally using this talk and noticing his being reassured, but as that paragraph develops with intimate details of Lena's and Einar's life, it becomes clear we've moved out of Lizette's head and into Einar's. We don't definitely go back to her POV until page 9 when "She studied his face." We stay with her through the end of the chapter.

In Chapter 2, we follow Lizette until page 13, when Sandy is looking at Lizette and obviously evaluating her, because Sandy snorts and we know why. In the next chapter, the POV moves somewhat randomly between Bomber and Rocket.

This is not necessarily an error. In many books the omniscient narrator hovers over the action and dialogue, dipping now into one character's intentions and perceptions, now into another's—sometimes with each new paragraph or line of dialogue—and the story moves forward on all fronts at whatever pace it needs to. But, as I said, I'm very sensitive to POV use and mechanics, so I found these changes unsettling.

I think that if you adopted a stricter use of POV—where we could see Einar from inside Lizette's head, then see Lizette from inside Einar's—you would have greater possibility for demonstrating her apparent craziness (from the outside) but her essential sanity (from inside), and his apparent thoughtlessness and possible senility (from the outside) but caring and sadness for his daughter (from inside).

Any book with multiple viewpoint characters, I believe, really benefits from strong POV control.

5. Final Thoughts

Writing action and adventure is relatively easy. We all climb the mountain in good fellowship—or know exactly who the enemies are. In a fight, Dave swings and Bill ducks. Andy shoots and, when the gun misfires, everyone knows it. Really straightforward.

Writing a novel of feelings is much harder. Jane Austen wrote novels of feeling, but I can't read them because they're all "tell." Consider the opening of *Sense and Sensibility*, where she lays the strictures on the family inheritance in less than a page. In the Emma Thompson movie script, we need multiple scenes where the half-brother and his scheming wife successively talk themselves down from a fair distribution of the estate to "helping out" the family every now and then. Modern writers simply cannot write things out plainly in direct discourse. Readers want and expect "show," not "tell."

Writing a novel of feelings is made even more difficult when people's relationships are awkward, like Lizette's and Einar's. And if the author is not in complete control of the text, it may be hard for the reader to know which parts are awkward because the emotional situation is awkward, and which are awkward because the text is tossing off mixed clues.

Writing feelings can be damned near impossible when you are trying to show—subtly, with finesse, with a caring heart (for Lizette is your main character, after all)—that Lizette may have painful memories and bizarre notions, or she may be mentally ill, although perhaps she is merely a private person dealing with a crushing load of stressful history. At the same time and in the same scenes, you are trying to suggest that Einar may be well meaning but emotionally stunted, or he may be an intellectual thief and monster, but now he's perhaps simply senile.

Similar awkward situations appear with Lizette and Sandy. Is Sandy, who's a box of tricks herself, going to use Lizette or kick her out? And with Rocket and Bomber. Just how stable and sustainable is this Animal House? And, unless I misunderstand, we haven't even met the Dogs yet!

With all of this going on, you need to exercise iron control as a writer. There's a lot of story happening in these first four chapters. I think some bits are getting away from you. For example, perhaps Rocket's musings and memories of Fisher and his piano playing in Chapter 3 could wait until a later chapter when Fisher actually appears. At the same time, we need to be a little clearer a little sooner about who these Dogs are and why they will be important to the story.

Even with POV control and the bias for "show," it's acceptable to pause occasionally inside the character's head to introduce the reader to situations, objects, and the backgrounds of other characters that the POV character already knows but without which the reader is lost. The POV style does not require the story flow to be an exact transcription of the thoughts and perceptions passing through the character's head in real time. The style just has to respect what he or she knows and what is hidden.

So, in my opinion, you need to:

1. Put some psychological distance between your knowledge of the story and what's actually written on the page.

2. Read with a fresh eye and iron out the little disjunctions that confuse the reader (like Einar's muscles and Rocket's eggs).

3. Decide what the POV character is or should be thinking or feeling in the moment and then reshape or discard any details and thoughts that conflict with or distract from this dominant mood or impression (like Rocket's basic competence).

4. If strict POV adherence works for you, think about recasting some of these chapters into two or more scenes. Chapter 1: (a) Lizette at the door, (b) Einar in the kitchen to start, (c) Lizette in the kitchen to finish and escaping the cuckoo clock. Chapter 2: (a) Lizette arriving at Sandy's and telling us about the street and who Sandy is, (b) Sandy in the laundry room, feeding her snake and scheming how to use or discard Lizette.

None of this calls for a major re-imagining of the story or where it's going. Instead, you want to do what I call a "snow-plow" or "steamroller" read: go through, push aside the loose stuff, and make the strong stuff stand out. You've got a fire hose of an imagination, now it's time to narrow and refine the stream.

Overall, I think you might have a book here that could stand alongside Ken Kesey's *Sometimes a Great Notion* or *One Flew Over the Cuckoo's Nest*. It will certainly find readers, especially among us Boomers who lived through the Sixties and wonder what the hell happened. (Don't discount the Boomers— sometimes I think we're the only people left who read for pleasure rather than play video games.)

Notes:

1. Pat Larkin (http://www.patricklarkin.net/) is another friend and former colleague. He specializes in historical, military, and espionage thrillers. His novel *The Tribune* is the first of a series set in imperial Rome at the time of Christ. He wrote two novels in Robert Ludlum's bestselling Covert-One series, *The Lazarus Vendetta* and *The Moscow Vector*. And earlier he coauthored with Larry Bond five novels of military fiction, including *Red Phoenix, Vortex, Cauldron, The Enemy Within,* and *Day of Wrath*.

2. Page numbers refer to the pre-published manuscript and do not correspond to the published version of *Adrift in the Sound*.

From: Kate
Sent: Thursday, August 18, 2011, 8:48 PM
Subject: Can't Wait to Get to Work!

Dear Tom:

I've looked at your edits of the first four chapters of *Adrift* and read your cover comments. I've been in the high Sierra today, hot and dusty, looking at how the landscape is recovering after timber clear cuts and watching the action at an experimental selected-timber logging site, taking lots of photos. I'm too tired now to do anything but say thank you, thank you!

You get what I'm trying to do with the story. You've provided insightful edits, precisely the kind of feedback I've been looking for. I see that your suggestions will help improve the narrative flow without blowing up the story. I can't wait to get to work on the changes and corrections, but will let them steep for a day or so and then get to it this weekend. I'm truly grateful for your wise counsel and constructive comments—and for the time you've so kindly given to my project. It's a real gift.

From: Tom
Sent: Friday, August 19, 2011, 12:07 PM
Subject: Just a Thought

Kate—

A further thought occurs to me. We suspect that Lizette has mental problems: the fact that she "just got out" of someplace, is unsure about the date, and her general air of dislocation and distance—but the latter could also be her reaction to her father. We need more clues to tell us she has problems.

One such clue comes up late in the interview, when she's suddenly aware of the cuckoo clock and afraid of its chiming. Right now, she comments internally on the clock because it doesn't fit the decor, and while that's an artistic judgment, it doesn't speak to her morbid fear that's only apparent at the end of the scene. Instead, make this clock one of the first things that she notices on coming into the kitchen ("The cuckoo clock still had its prominent place in his kitchen") and give us some reason to know that it's not just clocks or cuckoo clocks that are a problem but this one in particular in her family background: it was a source of disagreement between her artistic mother and stolidly intellectual father, or Einar would imitate the cuckoo to humiliate her when she misbehaved, or beat her in time to the chiming, or some other unhappy association. Then have her watch the clock apprehensively at least once more during the interview. The clock and her waiting for it to chime will provide tension—a countdown fuse—for what is otherwise simply an awkward meeting between estranged father and daughter. And the more irrational you make the associations with the clock, the more unstable we readers will judge her to be.

Just a thought. In general, when you find something that works symbolically or emotionally in a story, go back and find places to foreshadow it—forward for places to echo and enlarge on it—as a way of building dynamism into the conversations and actions.

———

From: Kate
Sent: Saturday, August 20, 2011, 10:29 AM
Subject: Nuts and Bugaboos

Hi Tom:

I've started changes and corrections to *Adrift* based on your very useful editing suggestions and think the beginning will be much improved thanks to your help. Your comments prompted some thoughts that I'd like to share, things I think about, but honestly don't have a place to express them without sounding like a complete nut. So, here goes:

POV (Point of View): This is a bugaboo I've been struggling with and appreciate, welcome your "Nazi" approach. I've probably read POV chapters in a dozen craft books and still don't have the hang of it. I took an advanced fiction class at University of California, Davis, with writer/teacher Sands Hall and she discussed POV, showed us examples in novelist/short story writer Jennifer Egan's work where she slid gracefully from one POV to another without clunky attributions. I want to learn to shift POV gracefully, seamlessly.

Your example of the knife fight in one of your stories is probably a sliding that works for both storyteller and reader. Until I get POV nailed down, I sincerely appreciate and need your disciplined approach, but will strain at the straitjacket, feel its confines, even after, like Houdini, I've broken free.

PROPS: You are right about Rocket's eggs in Cha. 3 and I'll fix it. In an earlier draft he sat down to eat them and the story went into an extraneous riff, which I cut, unfortunately the mechanics of eating the eggs went with it. The same for Einer's pipe smoking. It needs to be referenced in subsequent chapters and I've failed to do that. And, the concluding chapter must bring Watches Underwater back. The mask is there at the end, but I need for Lizette to touch it, put it on, make the symbolic connection tangible. I heard a rule-of-thumb during a panel discussion on writing last week at the Squaw Valley Community of Writers conference—for an object (symbol) to be real to the story it must appear at least three times. These seem like easy, mechanical fixes in *Adrift*.

CREATIVE CONTROL: I'm aware that my control is imperfect and I'm struggling to attain mastery. In a work of literature, in my view, there needs to be some looseness to make room for odd delights and atmospherics, but that does not mean lack of control. And, it's not an excuse for sloppy writing. I understand that every word must be "authorized" and that lyrical sequences and images must be apt. I'm getting better control, but it's far from an iron grip. In drafting *Adrift*, (funny word combination, if you say it out loud), I created images simply because I can and love to do it. Sometimes they amounted to sequences where I was showing off. Yes, they were beautiful or evocative. Did they move the narrative forward? No. Many have been cut, perhaps more need to go. The manuscript has been pared from about 120,000 words to about 88,000 now and I probably need to get it down to about 85,000, with some further plumping and cutting (final length: 92,000 words). My thinking is this: I can write vividly and with imagination, but need to be in control when I do, and I need to use this ability judiciously, not waste it. Readers need to come to my work, in part, because it's vivid and cinematic, lyricism spooned out, not shoveled on. I want readers to be hungry for more and need to guard against squandering this facility. I'm not there yet, but I'm working on it. Thanks for seeing that struggle for mastery in the work.

CHARACTERIZATIONS: Your comments here are troubling. You question the mental states of the characters: Is Lizette crazy or traumatized? Is Einar senile or grief stricken? Is Rocket dumb or smart? These ambiguities are intentional. I want the reader to wonder—and care enough to keep reading and find out. What troubles me is that the ambiguity might be a flaw that will turn the reader away before being resolved by the end of the story. Maybe readers won't care enough to find out! What I'm setting up is character development that leads to growth or change. (Not in Rocket's case, however, much to everyone's disappointment. In the end, he's just another dog, a dead orca.)

CONFLICT: Character changes from conflict are the crux of literary fiction, otherwise the reader might wonder "Why are you telling me this? So what?" I believe the answers to those questions are delivered at the end of *Adrift*. The question remains, however, can the reader live without tight character categorization in the beginning? My hope, in the words of writer/teacher Adair Lara,[1] who helped with a major structural revision of *Adrift,* is that I've "nailed" it in the end. We'll see. One person's opinion is just that. I'm praying she's right, but secretly think the ending needs a bit more creative muscle.

TASTE: One thing that has troubled me is the use of profane language in the book. I had a fiction Web site decline to publish an excerpt of *Adrift* because the editors deemed it "inappropriate" for their readers. I've agonized about the language, checked every swear word, weighed it to see if it was necessary. I've wandered around the house in my pajamas at 3 AM muttering cuss words in dialog to make sure it works and that it's authentic to the characters. There are 15 f-bombs in *Adrift*. I've evaluated each one and decided that it must stay to maintain the authenticity of speech. Likewise, I've looked at the other profanities and vulgarisms, knowing there are some readers who will reject the story on those grounds.

Novelist John Steinbeck wrote to Pat Covici that one of the most dangerous suggestions editors make is a change based on some bias about good taste. At the time, Steinbeck was resisting pressure from editors and publisher to change the ending to *Grapes of Wrath* where Rose of Sharon offers her milk-heavy breast to a starving stranger. Steinbeck called the notion of taste a codification of manners and attitudes of the past, ignoring that originality itself is bad taste because it departs from the collective norm.

He said: "I might go so far as to believe that any writer who produced a book of unquestioned good taste has written a tasteless book … because there is no taste in life nor in nature. It is simply the way it is." I have presented the Dogs as they are and appreciate that you haven't objected to their vulgar speech and street vernacular. They are who they are, but still I worry about their language and whether readers will be put off by it.

There's much more in your insightful comments that have caused me to reflect on what I'm doing. I'm not resisting your suggestions or justifying flaws. Far from it. I'm thinking about what you've said, savoring each observation to figure out how it can help the work, help the story. I sincerely need and appreciate this conversation. Thanks, again.

Notes:

1. Adair Lara is an award-winning San Francisco newspaper columnist and memoirist who teaches writing and offers book consulting services.

From: Tom
Date: Sunday, August 20, 2011, 1:23 PM
Subject: Re: Some Thoughts While Editing

Kate—

I've put my responses in a Word document, easier and faster for me to write and edit than an email. You raise good points. Here are my thoughts.

[Attachment]

Tom's Reply to Kate's August 20 Email

General Disclaimer: I never actually had creative writing courses (maybe one in college, and by then I'd written a complete novel) or much contact with professionals, other than working alongside Pat Larkin and discussing his books and mine on a regular basis. I also collaborated with David Drake (http://david-drake.com/) on one book in a science fiction trilogy, where the other two junior authors were Bill Dietz (http://williamcdietz.com/home.html) and Roger McBride Allen (http://www.sff.net/people/roger.allen/); with Roger Zelazny (http://www.roger-zelazny.com/) on two books, and with Frederik Pohl (http://www.frederikpohl.com/) on one. These collaborations were arm's length affairs, where the publisher arranged the deal and didn't want the junior author, me, pestering the senior author with phone calls, chat, and questions.

I picked up a few things from seeing their notes and early drafts, though. But I'm really mostly self-taught. Every writer is self-taught: you learn what works for you. No one can teach anyone how to write, just offer a few suggestions about what works for them.

POV: I found this a natural way of writing. I do scenes from a single POV pretty much the way movies are cut into scenes: specific actions with beginning, middle, end. You're doing it in chapters, I break chapters down into smaller scenes.[1]

Always, in the first paragraph or before the first line of dialogue, I have to establish whose viewpoint we're sharing. For me this is now easy: I just toss in a memory, reflection, or observation from the POV character buffered by "it seemed to Adam" or similar wording. Since I usually need a "downbeat" to start a scene—that is, a thought, an image, a sensory cue like a smell, or some other natural starting point—it's even easier to place this cue within the POV character's perception.

If you don't employ strict scene control, as I choose to do, then you need to mark the shift. You're right: you don't want to do it in a heavy-handed or obvious manner ("Now let's hear it from Einar's point of view ..."), but neither do you want the shift so subtle that the reader misses it. When we go into Einar's head for his reflections about his wife, you could start that paragraph with: "As his daughter talked about paint and canvas, Einar was reassured ..." Since Lizette would not be likely to refer to herself as "his daughter," it marks the transition point. (And of course, you need to mark the move back in similar fashion.)

For me, the simplest way to think of POV is "first person narrative told in third person." As an exercise, write that first scene in first person: "... Einar spoke to me through the screen door ... I stood at the bottom of the stairs and watched my father ..." and you can identify who "I" is by having the first line of dialogue be: " 'So, Lizette ... you're here.' " Get everything right in first person, which will naturally show up any errors if you write about things she doesn't, can't, or wouldn't know. It will also place you as the writer firmly in her head and make it easy to identify feelings, reactions, con-clusions, etc. Then go through the text—line by line, not with find/replace—and change "I" to Lizette and "me" or "my" to "her" accordingly, turning first person narrative into third person.

Practice like this will give you a strong feel for POV.

Creative Control: This doesn't mean you can't toss off things as they happen around the characters. If you describe the mossy stones in a brook your character is crossing, that doesn't mean he or she has to slip on them, or that someone has to pick one up and throw it. There's nothing here that's "authorized."

But you have to be aware at all times of what the reader is see-ing, sensing, and supposing. If your character dances lightly across those stones, your reader will hold in mind a person who's surefooted. If the character then trips and stumbles on bare ground, there had better be an obvious explanation like a loose rock or root. Your character can't be surefooted one minute and a klutz the next. If the stumble is just some piece of stage business that occurs to you right now—("and then he fell down")—that's loss of control.[2]

The reader's perceptions exist in the focal point of a spotlight that you control. You are Virgil leading Dante into Hell, and he sees only whatever you raise your lantern beside to show it. When I was working on my second book, back in the 1970s, I read an interview with Marilyn Durham, the author of *The Man Who Loved Cat Dancing*. She said the hardest thing for her to learn was how to get a character through a door. I had struggled with a similar issue in writing my first book back in high school. Do you describe the wooden panels, the mold-ings, the paint, the knob? Does the character have to turn the knob? Does the opening door have to make a sound?

Her solution was you don't open a door unless what's behind it is important. (My solution, taken from that, is you usual-ly don't even have to make the character enter or leave the room; the scene begins and ends there.) If you focus on the door, you give it importance: who or what is waiting there. You might describe the door to give an indication of the age, condition, and so on of the house and by extension the char-acter of the people living in it. But if you're getting a character into a room, "he opened the door" is sufficient and may not even be necessary—"he entered the room."

Characterization: This again is a blend of what the reader sees and believes (cross cutting always with what the reader knows to be real from his or her own life experience). It is very difficult to show a character through action and leave it as a mystery as to what his or her true nature is.

You give a strong cue at the beginning of the first scene, with Lizette having "gotten out"—from where is presumably left to be discovered; from some kind of custody, either jail or hospitalization, is supposed. (We can guess Einar is probably not talking about a bad marriage or a temporal vortex.) Both jails and hospitals are time-conscious places ("your hearing date is on the 13th," "you'll talk with the doctor on Friday"), so the fact that she is unaware of the current date is an immediate tipoff to the fact that she's dissociated from reality. It's not a diagnosis of schizophrenia or bipolar yet, but a solid clue. It's okay then to also have her be perceptive and aware. Crazy people don't babble or see things in a daze—unless they're in a psychotic state, and then all bets are off.

As a reader, I accepted the ambiguity about Lizette. Maybe insane, maybe traumatized, jury still out, okay, watch for further clues. But now, as a writer, you are walking a path with cliffs on either side. You need to keep feeding me clues—sane stuff, not-so-sane stuff—or I'm going to start taking Lizette at face value and wonder what that first scene was all about. Lizette can help out here by sometimes doubting her own sanity—the reality of her own memories and current perceptions—through internal dialogue. People who are mentally ill are not oblivious to their condition.

Rocket is a harder situation. Smart or stupid is a less interesting dichotomy for the reader to deal with. The reader takes pretty much for granted the basic intelligence of any character you show. If he's a genius, we want a concerto or a physics theorem introduced up front. If he's dumb, we want an obvious example through dialogue that doesn't quite mesh or a stupid stunt. Showing that people are fit for some situations but not for others must be consistently supported by POV and internal dialogue.

Rocket can show basic urban squatter survival instincts in the scenes in the Dogs' house, but when he gets on the boat, he needs to start explaining himself. "… he knew the slow start was his fault, but time had a habit of getting away from Rocket." If he's reading a children's book using his finger, "… Rocket didn't read many books, but he liked this one on dolphins and whales, even if it was basically for kids, because he found the huge creatures fascinating. He knew of them from sightings in the sound, and loved their grace and majesty. If he had gone farther in school—which for Rocket pretty much stopped in the seventh grade—he might have become a marine biologist and studied them for a living. As it was, he just wanted to watch them and pick up new facts where he could."

It's okay to "tell" background like this without engineering a way of showing it. The passage above about books is what I mean by *internal dialogue*: text from the POV of the character taking us inside his head and his history. Your writing classes might have called this something else, but "internal dialogue" works for me.

Again, you can—in fact, must—let the character evolve for the reader: seems pretty smart at home, but not a good worker or terribly dependable, not much schooling but plenty of empathy, not sure I like him yet, but I know people like that. My main trouble with Rocket on the reading was he changed too much, too quickly between Chapter 3 and Chapter 4. I didn't get inside him.

To follow Adair Lara's thought, however: if you "nail" him in the end, then every fact or supposition the reader's gotten about Rocket has to fit. You don't want the reader coming to that end and saying, "Yeah, but on page 23 …" Wrapping it up means no loose ends, and that's when the writer is in control.

Matters of Taste: Yes, this is a hard one.[3] As always, the language your characters use must fit their situation, their understanding, their class and upbringing—everything that makes a person distinctive. And the elements of the story, like Rose of Sharon's breast, must fit the vision out of which you're writing.

Crude and violent characters must be … well, crude and violent. It would be disconcerting and false if a hardened Chicago gangster were to yell, "Shut up, you mean guy!" or "Golly, I missed that shot!" But, with that said, most of us—especially experienced, older readers—don't relish spending a lot of time with foul-mouthed characters of limited vocabulary whose all-purpose adjective, verb, and noun begins with "F." Some current movies and television, as well as novels by less experienced authors, are so laced with profanity—in pursuit of somebody's idea of reality—that they're virtually impenetrable.

In my own writing, I tend toward characters who are more educated, enlightened, and thoughtful as people with whom *I* can identify. Sometimes, also, they are coming from an entirely different time, culture, or dimension. So I try to save profanity for moments of extreme stress and wonderment, and usually get to put it in a foreign language.

When using the "first person in third person" narrative style, it would also be appropriate to tone down the profanity. Yes, people often think in the same terms they use when speaking, but the sensing human mind does not always comment self-consciously—and with colorful language—on its own thoughts and perceptions. Even a foul-mouthed, lower-class gangster can simply see, hear, and think without immersion in f-words.

Notes:

1. In proofing the scans that Principled Technologies made for Baen's ebook of *Crygender,* I found that they had lumped the last scene of the last chapter (separated by a linespace) in with the scene that went before. The action continued dialogue where one character was reading another his constitutional rights during an arrest, and in the final scene of about three paragraphs the arrestee was hearing his rights and internally debating whether to resist (of which he was eminently capable) or submit. He decided to submit. I corrected the proof to make this a separate action. Their proofer undid my correction. The book on the Baen site has a continuous scene. In other distributions, I restored the separation. To me, this stuff is important.

2. In *Flare,* which I wrote with Roger Zelazny, a character in an aircar crashes into a lake and struggles with his seatbelt as the cabin fills with water. Roger made very few comments on my draft, but he did note that the character had not buckled in before takeoff. I checked and the buckling in was there, but obviously not strong enough for

a reader to notice and remember. I added a word or two so that the act stood out more prominently. That's how closely people read our works.

3. And yes, I'm conscious that I used an f-bomb in referring to Rocket as a "fuckup." But that would be language appropriate to his situation on the tugboat.

From: Kate
Sent: Sunday, August 21, 2011, 10:04 AM
Subject: Tick-tock and Collisions

Dear Tom:

With your help, I've completed re-editing the first 25 pages of *Adrift* and feel like the work is solid, but I've gained about 1,000 words. I'm not obsessive about word count, I'm just trying to keep the manuscript at a good commercial length. But, I feel more confident about the novel's launch and appreciate your focus on the needs of the reader. Damn readers who need A, B, C in logical sequence. It's more fun to write all over the place and trust Dear Reader will figure it out. Cheesh!

I checked with my Puget Sound tow-boat expert and you are right, an orca, even a beefy 10-ton specimen, would not lift a tug out of a wave trough. However, big logs, which litter the Sound, will cause a slight list when they're run over. The problem is not the lurching of the boat, but potential damage to the hull and prop. When a tug hits a big log, they do stop and check for damage, but rarely find serious problems with structure and mechanics, although it happens.

I've heightened the tick-tock of the cuckoo clock because you're right, it can be used to heighten dramatic tension. Lizette is caught by her Dad and wants to get away. I hope I've effectively presented it that way and it puts pressure on the scene. And, I've worked on Rocket based on your comments, wised him up a bit, softened him. In my view, he's a simple guy with a good heart, but corrupted by drugs.

I've invested about 17 hours this weekend in the revisions and corrections and know the opening is stronger. I also hope, based on your pointers, that I'll be better able to see the logic faults, clumsy point of view shifts, and inconsistencies in the next 25 pages. I was blind to them before. Thanks so much for your help.

P.S. Based on your emails to me, I'm seeing a book on craft from you. Yes, there are thousands of books on writing. The same is true of diet books, which sell like sno cones at a summer Weight Watchers convention. Sometimes it takes the right voice or the right logic to see how to put the nuts and bolts together. I really got serious about completing *Adrift* after I read detective story writer Walter Mosley's *This Year You Write Your Novel*. Mosley gave me a kick in the pants to either get serious about my writing or get over it.

From: Tom
Sent: Sunday, August 21, 2011, 10:14 AM
Subject: Blacksmithing

Kate—

I'm glad to hear the work is going well and flattered to think I may have been of help. Writing something really strong, then corralling the various parts of the book and making them work right is one of the most satisfying things in my life. I think of it in physical terms, like blacksmithing—hammering out the bent parts, making lovely curves, sharpening edges—except it's all in the mind.

As I've written elsewhere—I think also in an email to Elizabeth—writing fiction is like being God to a palm-sized universe. You don't really know who you are until you've written a novel.

We'll have more to talk about when we meet on the 3rd.

From: Kate
Sent: Sunday, September 4, 2011, 4:58 PM
Subject: Translations from Chinese

Dear Tom:

Thank you for the stimulating discussion yesterday at Elizabeth's and for your support of our book projects. I'm excited about Elizabeth's debut and look forward to getting *Adrift* into shape for publishing. I appreciate your generous offer to provide a final edit.

I was so stimulated after our meeting that I did a couple of hours of editing last night, then got up at 3:30 AM and continued until now, with a 2-hour break for yoga. I have attached the next five chapters of *Adrift,* about 50 pages. I understand that you have a lot of irons in the fire and know that you will look at this section as your time and other priorities permit, which is to say there is no pressure from me. I don't expect the same depth of editing as with the first 25 pages, that would be too much to ask, really.

In *Adrift,* I'm working with a limited omniscient narrator, but have taken your POV discipline to heart and hope the flow from one character point of view to the another is smooth, logical, and in keeping with your strictures. I believe that your approach is a benefit to the reader and I want to be disciplined in my use of POV for the reader's sake. At this point, I'm not sure I see things anymore. I take things out, put them back in, change, change back.

What I hope most of all is that reading *Adrift* is enjoyable for you. If you feel like the manuscript reads like the Chinese translation of a software manual, I'm sunk.

And, I hope there will be ways I can be helpful to you with your projects. I would like to read *The Judge's Daughter,* which sounds like a departure in genre for you. Since I don't have an ereader, would you email me a copy of the manuscript so I can see your new direction?

I feel like we laid a good foundation for getting support for our collective writing and publishing efforts and hope we will be able to work together to bring our projects to market and generate audience interest and sales. It was so good to see you. Thanks.

From: Kate
Sent: Monday, September 5, 2011, 10:21 AM
Subject: Pressure Cooking

Hi Elizabeth:

Thanks so much for a stimulating day on Saturday and for the delicious lunch. I'm jazzed. I left your house with a head full of ideas that pressure-cooked all the way home. When I got in that night, I spent a couple of hours re-editing *Adrift*, then got up at 3:30 AM and got back to it. By 5 PM Sunday, with a 2-hour break for yoga, I had 50 pages ready to ship and sent them to Tom. I hope he doesn't feel overwhelmed by my actions.

My sense is that Tom is encouraging me to be a better self-editor and he wants to protect his time by getting me to clean up as much as possible before he sees it. This seems very sensible to me. I want to be respectful of his time and use his editing skills to best advantage for both of us—and be more self-sufficient in editing my own work.

I contacted my graphic designer/photographer friend, Matt Salvo (http://www.mattsalvo.com), this morning, asking for his help with the chapter icons. I told him I think 8 to 9 icons will work. Finish size for chapter headings might be 2x2 inches. I've gone online and was surprised to find a number of clip-art images of Pacific Northwest Native American designs similar to what I have in mind. The icons might be easier to create than I thought. But, I'm no expert in design.

Icons I think are needed to make the concept work in the book's design:

Lizette—main character, symbol: "Watches Underwater," mask with full, sensual lips, sexy, strong, mysterious

Marian—midwife, symbol: medicine stick or wand

Sandy—exotic dancer, stripper, symbol: snake, perhaps swallowing prey, erotic

Rocket—tugboat sailor, symbol: orca (killer whale) leaping, maybe with man riding

Poland—Native American ranch manager, symbol: dancing (circular) salmon

The Dogs—strung out guys who crash at Rocket's house, symbol: scary, mean totem (stacked faces), dog

Raven—Native American soldier, son of Poland and his wife Abaya, symbol: Raven

Violet—beautiful infant, symbol: hummingbird, flower (something delicate and beautiful)

Greg—Marian's junkie boyfriend, a real butthead, symbol: mangy wolf or snarling coyote

There was some discussion Saturday after my suggestion about icons that they might be worked into the cover design, perhaps an image of the mask "Watches Underwater" in vibrant colors might work. This mask, however, is complete fiction and is not part of the Native American cultural tradition or design motifs. The icon images also could be used on the book's Web site and in marketing materials. Maybe prints, posters, mugs, and T-shirts could be sold with icons on them, how the heck do I know?

As you can see, I'm very inspired by your lead and generous offer to help launch *Adrift in the Sound*. I'd like to get the manuscript to you before you go to Hawaii so you can look it over as time permits. You'll be on vacation, after all, perhaps not the best time to pick a manuscript apart.

I'm excited by the upcoming debut of *Jackie,* can't wait to buy copies and give them to friends, and I'm energized by the prospects for my own book. Thank you so much for your support, kindness and inspiration, not to mention your and Lee's hospitality.

From: Tom
Sent: Monday, September 5, 2011, 10:45 AM
Subject: Re: Thanks for a Wonderful Saturday

Kate—

For both the chapter heads and cover design icons, think in any size that seems convenient to the designer. They can then be reduced to the appropriate page size with In-Design. But for your ebook, they'll want to be on the order of 100-200 pixels across, for fast loading; so you don't want the designs too intricate or feathery. Woodcut is about the right level.

I do advocate self-editing most strongly—not just to protect my time, but as an exercise in thinking like the reader. Also, cheaper in the long run.

Elizabeth—

Thanks for hosting the day, with a delicious lunch. Good luck with the launch of the Jackie book.

From: Kate
Sent: Monday, September 5, 2011, 11:10 AM
Subject: Graphics

Tom—

Excellent advice. I'll include your comments in discussion with graphic designer, if I get that far. Thanks.

From: Kate
Sent: Thursday, September 8, 2011, 5:52 AM
Subject: Marketing Tips

Hi Tom:

Found this interesting guide for creating Facebook marketing campaigns ["My Facebook Formula" PDF available from eReleases®]. You may already have a Facebook marketing plan, but this guide might have some helpful tips you haven't seen.

From: Tom
Sent: Thursday, September 15, 2011, 5:18 PM
Subject: My Edits – Still Willing to Read

Kate—

Here are my edits and comments. Sorry it's taken so long, but I'm also struggling with my own book.

In some places I did a little reworking, rather than try to suggest changes. Three general observations:

(1) After Lizette goes to the island, we get a lot of her backstory in dream sequences (the rape) and either dreams or flashbacks (the hospitalization and interview with Dr. Finch). The pace of the story is already pretty slow at this point, seems to be drifting with Lizette. You might consider how important these are. For chronology, you might even want to start the book with the rape (start with a good, dramatic, gripping action scene) and then medical hospitalization that turns into a 5150 situation—then have her go home to her father and pick up her checks in order to find something about who she is.

(2) I know a thing or two about mental illness from almost 20 years of volunteering at NAMI (National Alliance on Mental Illness). Between the late '60s-early '70s and today there has been a real change in treatment of mental illness. Many more medications are now targeted to certain symptoms (see the pamphlet on my site http://www.thomastthomas.com/Medications_for_Mental_Health_2011.pdf), and there was a move away from Freudian talk therapy toward medication exclusively (prescribe and goodbye), and now practice is turning back to a combination of medication and talk therapy with emphasis on wellness and recovery. There was also a change in the way people were committed and examined, starting with Lanterman-Petris-Short in California (1967) and the Involuntary Treatment Act in Washington (1972). Per my comments in the scene, you need to be sure what rules or conventions governed commitment in 1971 [actually, this should be 1973, the year in which *Adrift* is set] and try to follow them—your authorities would.

In those years, I'm not sure Dr. Finch would speak so casually about Lizette being able to live a normal life if she was diagnosed with schizophrenia or something similarly grave.

That's a very modern viewpoint. And even if it's not completely accurate, the doctor would still have to make a diagnosis if she has prescribed a medication regimen. And some of the first-generation medications, like Thorazine, probably wouldn't be given outside a hospital setting anyway.

You can probably finesse not giving a diagnosis for a lot of readers, but some of your readers will be drawn to the book precisely because it portrays mental illness. This becomes tricky, because "schizoaffective disorder"—a kind of cycling schizophrenia, or a borderline case between the psychosis of schizophrenia and the mania of bipolar—is a relatively recent diagnosis. Although "schizoaffective psychosis" was first coined in 1933, a lot of disease definitions were still fluid through the 1950s and into the 1960s. Some psychiatrists were still using "dementia praecox" to refer to schizophrenia symptoms in the '50s. You might want to see if you can get a copy of DSM-II (*Diagnostic and Statistical Manual of Psychology, Second Edition*—we're now on Fifth Edition), which would reflect thinking of the psychiatric community in your timeframe, to support what Dr. Finch is saying and a preliminary diagnosis of Lizette.

(3) As a reader, I don't much like these people. The Dogs don't even rise to the level of "bears with furniture" (to quote an old definition of most young male bachelors). Rocket is okay, but still pretty cold to drop her in the middle of downtown with hardly a goodbye. Cadillac Carl is vermin and Greg not much better, although he hasn't killed anyone yet. Lizette is the most sympathetic character until she scrubs the toilet with Greg's toothbrush just 'cause she doesn't like him. (I call that real passive-aggressive—way too aggressive and only passive because she does it without telling him.) Marian seems the most stable and giving, although she seems to be struggling with latent lesbianism—and how does that play out with her young, straight mothers? Poland (from what I've seen so far) is the most grounded. I don't necessarily have to identify with the people in the stories I read, but I need some reason to like them in order to care about them. Is this coming soon?

But still willing to read more from you ...

From: Kate
Sent: Thursday, September 15, 2011, 5:18 PM
Subject: Re: Chapters 5-10

Dear Tom:

You are right on the money—in terms of timing the edits to me and your observations. I did not send this section to you with any preface, just let go and held my breath. I feared (probably knew) the flashbacks are too long and slow down the narrative. I've been whittling them down—they were chapters that I've tried to condense, but obviously not enough. I did have the rape chapter earlier in the narrative, but the story started with the Dogs and then moved to the rape. Adair suggested restructuring, saying the rape came too soon in the story, but I may not have done a smooth job of reknitting the narrative (I'm such a rookie). That's where I've felt I really needed your help, have worked on those sections for too long without seeing what needs to be fixed. Your critical eye is a godsend. I haven't looked at your edits yet, but know your observations will really help. I'm grateful and I'm probably about to become even more so.

I'm sorry about the Dogs—they *are* worse than animals. It's one of the underlying premises of the book: What happens to the earth, happens to the children of the earth. When the earth is degraded, we are all degraded. I will tell you truly that the Dogs existed. I was casually acquainted with them and their disgusting crash pad and I've tried to render them accurately. Only a few of them are still alive today, and the survivors are in pretty bad shape. I've spoken with a couple of them at various times as I've been writing the book to try and capture the milieu. I believe the way I've presented the scene is spot-on.

1973, a time of great transition, proceeded from the free drugs, free love, anything goes 60s, but as Bob Dylan said "the times they are a changin'," and in reality many of the drifters didn't make it into the new era. Remember that I grew up in San Francisco a few blocks from Golden Gate Park, graduated from high school in 1967 right into the Summer of Love. I've known a lot of people whose minds were blown, who overdosed, committed suicide, who became zombies or didn't come out alive.

The toothbrush thing has gotten generally good response from early readers—female. The feedback was that Lizette has been wandering around like a victim. What she does to Greg shows Lizette getting stronger and starting to fight back. I had several readers say they felt like cheering after she did it—one woman wrote on the review copy "Go, Lizette, go!" Lizette's action may evoke different responses, based on gender. That, however, doesn't address your concern about character motivation, which I know is important in believable fiction. I'll look at Lizette's action with that in mind.

The bathroom scene with Lizette and Marian reflects the lack of sexual boundaries common in the 1960s hippie scene. John Lennon sang "Whatever gets you through the night." But the relationship between the two women is more loving than nighttime sexual antics. It's about Marian reconnecting Lizette to her own feminine essence, sensing the damage of the rape, but not really knowing what happened. I believe the scene is important, but I want to present it in a way that transcends the strictures of homosexuality as we define it today—it's more about what feels good and comforting than firm sexual preference. My preference is to leave it in.

Although the Stonewall Riots in New York were in 1969, gay rights really took off in 1973 when the American Psychiatric Association removed homosexuality from its official list of mental disorders (DSM) and job hiring and firing rules began to change. Harvey Milk ran for San Francisco city supervisor in 1973, but didn't win that time, although he got huge national media attention as the first openly homosexual political candidate. If the bath scene doesn't work, doesn't reflect the blurring of boundaries in the era that ushered in a wider definition of sexuality, doesn't impart the intimacy and caring between the two women, it's going to have to be reworked or come out, but I don't want to cut it if I can help it.

You got me on Lizette's mental illness—I see it as undefined, presenting various symptoms that could be one thing or another—mania, depression, disaffective disorder, catatonia, belligerent, unruly, disoriented, distant, borderline personality disorder (which is new, and perhaps a catchall). I don't want to say she's manic depressive or autistic or schizophrenic. I'm unsure that Thorazine is the right medication for her and worried about it not being right, but not one of the dozen or so readers of earlier drafts questioned the prescription.

But, you're right. A wider audience for the story will include readers far more versed in mental illness than me.

Another reason you are such a benefit to this story is that you know and question. I knew a woman in the late-1970s who took lithium for bi-polar disorder, which I think was a very new drug at the time, so I don't know that it would have been available to Lizette. I will do some research this weekend, checkout your Web site. What I'm looking for is a vague diagnosis and a prescription that will even Lizette out so she functions more smoothly. I don't want to get too clinical. She seems to only get whacked out when under stress or fear. I believe in the right circumstances she will function near normal. She'd better, because she's going to need her wits for responsibilities that come later in the story.

I'm glad you like Poland and Abaya. I love them. Adair said she thinks they're almost *too* good and that I should rough them up a bit. I've tried. Abaya is sassier, more conniving, and Poland more judgmental than in earlier versions. They represent the cultural/environmental constant, the glue that keeps the tribe, the nation, the world together. They have not been corroded by sex, drugs, and rock 'n' roll, by fashion and material things. They live simply and honestly. They're not pop culture, like Andy Warhol.

I hope you're going to like what's coming next, it's gentler and sweeter as Lizette heals. But then it's back to Seattle and the Dogs, but not as rough this time, promise, maybe even fun. You've seen more than enough of those guys to get the picture of how wasted they are. I assure you, there were thousands of young people in the same boat during those years—lost, wasted, out of their minds. Walking wounded wandering the streets. No one talks about the carnage of the Cultural Revolution. They talk about the rock concerts and tripping around, flowers in your hair, getting high, everything feelin' groovy. Yeah, right. Change exacts a dear price.

As I've said, and I'm quite sincere, I want to be respectful of your writing time. I know you'll get to the story when you can. You've sent me plenty to work on in the meantime. I would like to send you Chapters 11 through 15 (44 pages) by the end of the weekend. I've been working on this project, in between work and taking care of family, for four years. There's no reason to rush now. Please know that I am very grateful for your help. I've gotten to the place with the manuscript where I can't see the forest for the trees. Your insights are invaluable. It's Zen: When the student is ready, the teacher will appear. What matters most in the end is that the story serves the reader. Thanks.

From: Tom
Sent: Friday, September 16, 2011, 11:50 AM
Subject: Some Responses

(1) I can understand about your not wanting to give a formal diagnosis. Lizette with her flightiness, occasional violence, etc. would have been a puzzle in any period of diagnostics. But I would always object to a psychiatrist sending her off with a bottle of pills and essentially saying "have a nice life." If the doctors can't find a diagnosis, they might try some meds while she's in the hospital (diagnosis by prescription), but a couple of weeks is way too fast for any psychotropic medication to work (usually takes six weeks or more just to have an effect).

(2) Dr. Finch would not be at a state to tell Lizette that just by taking these pills she would be able to live a normal life. And certainly not if they're Thorazine—which was essentially a fast-acting, high-impact med used to calm psychotic patients into a zombie-like state, easier to manage in a hospital setting. That's why it's important to know the then-current laws on restraint: Dr. Finch may be forced to let Lizette go, even though she's been unable to find a diagnosis and can't guarantee any kind of cure or path to stability. If the doctor is her friend, or trying to be, then Finch should be regretful about all this, not "take your pills, run along, examine your life, and stay out of trouble."

(3) I understand about the free-swinging '60s, although I didn't personally take part. However, you'll be introducing your book into a culture where homosexuality and LGBT issues are now widely debated and politicized. Maybe you need to subtly quote those Lennon lyrics or something to remind us that people in the subculture were more casual then about sex in all its forms. Also, because it's unclear whether Rocket

and Lizette's sleeping together was just friendly, brother-sister-type nesting or outright casual uncommitted sex, and that this so far has been the only other sex in the book, the situation with Marian needs more padding and buffering.

(4) Greg has, so far, been just an uncaring and sometimes leering lout. We've been given no reason for him to be singled out for enemy action like the toothbrush retaliation. That Lizette stoops to it puts her character in doubt. In general, I am sensitive to, and dislike, passive-aggressive tactics. They smack of sneakiness, basic dishonesty, and cowardice: "I want to do you harm, but I don't want to provoke an actual confrontation, where I might lose. Instead, I'll do something that, if I'm ever caught and challenged, I can deny." Perhaps women like passive-aggressive tactics against men because they can do damage without provoking a male fight response and a black eye. But it's still, in my mind, a character weakness. Strong people defend themselves openly or put aside the cause of anger. Can you imagine the centered Poland or Abaya doing this to Greg's toothbrush?

If Lizette is someone I'm supposed to like, she can be hurt and trampled in her weakness at the opening of the book, then work her way to real strength, personal mastery and salvation, by the end. This petty action is a stumbling block on that path.

(5) So far, aside from the home values of Marian, Poland, and Abaya—which draw from a time and tradition far older than the '60s—all you've shown us is the breakup and decay of the '70s. If your book is really going to show this group and this setting as a period of transition, then there has to be some semi-sweet, bitter-sweet but still palpable, echo of the good things about the summer of love. Even this early in the book, the characters have to make some internal reference to how much easier, freer, more copacetic, more loving their situation used to be. You've got a hint of this in Marian's reference to the young hippie couple who build their place high up the mountain. We need more of these contrasts to show your theme. Otherwise we start off in confusion and despair and then go ... where?

From: Kate
Sent: Friday, September 16, 2011, 12:06 PM
Subject: Wow! More to Chew On

I see your well-taken points and like the way your mind sparkles, but also see a good bit of work for me to address these issues and strengthen the story. I want to make the needed changes gracefully and improve the flow, so it will take me a while to sort things out and get the positioning right. You are amazing and I'm lucky.

From: Kate
Sent: Sunday, September 18, 2011, 5:21 PM
Subject: Keeping Time

Here is the next batch of chapters. I've been working on timelines—the novel timeline for keeping my narrative time sequence consistent and accurate. It's attached because it might help you to keep me honest and the novel on track.

The timeline of major events in 1973 might work as an addition at the back of the book to provide context for the reader. A friend suggested writing a preface to the novel that discusses the social/political context for the book, but that sounds kind of academic for fiction. I'm just collecting factoids right now and know the timeline is too long and needs editing. I just want to know what you think of the idea?

Because I have a lot of work to do on chapters 5 through 10 that you returned, there's no rush to get these new chapters edited. When you find time in coming weeks will be great. As always, thanks for your help.

From: Tom
Sent: Monday, September 19, 2011, 8:57 AM
Subject: Novels Are Not Textbooks

Where did I get the impression that the book was in 1971? "It's mid-January, 1973" right there on the first page. Anyway, since the ITA was passed in 1972, you really need to find the original language of the legislation and work your story of Lizette's hospitalization against its terms. Dr. Finch might even make a reference to the new law and how it keeps her from holding Lizette for further treatment. ... Sorry to confuse things by my mis-remembering of the dates.

In general, I don't think novels are helped by bits of academia like prefaces and timelines. (Unless they are ironically part of the story—in, say, a novel about academics.) A preface about what you're trying to show is always suspect: if the book doesn't carry the theme sewn into its fabric, a preface won't help. Storytelling is the art of weaving it all together.

As to a timeline of outside events at the end ... Instead you might put that at the beginning, in place of a preface, to remind the reader of what 1973 was like and set the context of the outside world. But most of these events might be better woven into the story of the character's lives, their realizations and impacts on their thinking. Giving this timeline feels like packing the book with your research, rather than using it in your story. And some events—like Lexis/Nexis, the first cell phone, stone skipping, and Spiro Agnew—aren't going to have much impact or effect on your characters anyway. I generally believe the story should start, traverse, and end, and that's your statement.

The one time I consciously broke with that was in *First Citizen*,[1] when I introduced recent Constitutional amendments at the beginning of the book. These were events that would have a profound effect on Granny and Billy's lives, but would have taken too much of a sidetrack to introduce at the appropriate point in the story. So I put them up front, with appropriate dates, and gave Granny a commentary—thereby establishing him as soon to become a national figure. Everything else—like the nuking of Washington, DC—was woven into the characters' stories.

Notes:

1. Thomas also broke with this rule in the book he then had in production, *The Children of Possibility* (published March 2012). Because that story involves unique concepts in time travel and specialized usage of common terms, the front matter includes a dictionary fragment from the 102nd century and excerpts from the handbook of the far-future travelers.

From: Kate
Sent: Wednesday, September 21, 2011, 7:34 PM
Subject: Twists and Turns

Hi Elizabeth & Tom:

If you aren't aware of "The Book of Publishing" by Keith Gessen in the new *Vanity Fair* magazine, it's the best insider look at the current state of book publishing I've seen. The story follows the publication of one book—*The Art of Fielding* by Chad Harbach—which is coming out now, and the piece goes through the twists and turns of the New York publishing industry, describing the confused, troubled, and unpredictable world of U.S. book publishing in the age of big retailers and ereaders.

An extended version of the magazine story "How a Book is Born: The Making of the Art of Fielding" is available for ereaders at http://www.vanityfair.com/magazine/ebooks. I highly recommend it.

From: Tom
Sent: Thursday, September 22, 2011, 10:02 AM
Subject: Thanks

I'll look into it. FYI, I've got the fourth of my blogs on Gutenberg vs. eBooks up now on my Web site (with the other three in the Blog Archive under "Various Art Forms.")

Pat Larkin's agent, Robert Gottlieb at Trident Media Group (http://tridentmediagroup.com/), sent him the attached clip from *Publishers Weekly*, which lays out the current market conditions. [The clipping showed that between 2010 and 2011, in a six-month period, printed book sales in all categories had declined by 22.9%, while ebook sales had increased 161.3%.] That was an introduction to an announcement, which Pat shared with me, about Trident's launching a digital publishing venture for its authors, details still to come. Gottlieb says they will offer "special deals and marketing not available to the average author uploading his manuscript on Amazon." Be interesting to see what that entails.

From: Kate
Sent: Thursday, September 22, 2011, 11:52 AM
Subject: Dog Piles

Thanks for the info. My fear with publishing anything is the marketing dog pile, my concern is how to loft a work out of the snapping mire so that potential readers can see it and make a fair decision about whether to buy. If Gottlieb has an answer, I'd like to know what it is. I'm not seeing a multimillion dollar ad campaign with all kinds of tie-ins in my future—Lizette action figures, mangled stuffed orca.

I'm listening, I'm looking for low-cost, high-impact marketing solutions. Isn't that what all this electronic jimcrackery is about? Pinpointing market opportunity at low-cost with lightening speed? God, I hate technology. Everybody talks all superior, like it's so hip and modern. In reality, it's like trying to do fancy needlework with a stick. Dog shit!

From: Tom
Sent: Thursday, September 22, 2011, 12:09 PM
Subject: My Experience

My experience has been that any focused online market you might tie into—in my case, discussion groups about science fiction or writing—already post multiple warnings about using your input there to sell yourself. They want you to come and schmooze about the topic, other authors, TV shows, and movies.

You can still use these places to market, but you have to invest a lot of time staying current with and contributing to the dominant discussion in order to squeak in a now-and-then reference to what you've done yourself. It's always a calculation of investment and return. I'm trying to go more broadly by making connections on Facebook and trying to inject a thought here and there. Don't know if it works yet. I've had a few sales and one subscriber so far.

From: Kate
Sent: Wednesday, September 28, 2011, 5:08 AM
Subject: Good News of Sorts

Dear Elizabeth & Tom:

Received notice that *Adrift in the Sound* is a semi-finalist in the Mercer Street Book Prize. Mercer Street Books is a big bookstore in New York's Greenwich Village, a hangout through the years for many famous writers and artists. Rick Rofihe is a short story writer whose work appears regularly in *The New Yorker* magazine. His online publishing business is http://www.anderbo.com/, which he claims gets a million hits a year.

The "prize" is $500 and an excerpt from the winning manuscript will be posted on the Anderbo Web site for six months. If *Adrift* were to win, the Anderbo Web site might be a good place to help generate pre-orders and sales once the book is published. I'm trying not to think about the contest, but want to thank you both for your support and quietly share my excitement.

Fortunately, Tom has edited and I have made changes to the manuscript for the sections called for in the contest: 8,000 words, 9,000 words. I'm very grateful for the help and know the editing made a difference, no matter the outcome of the contest. There is no indication of when the winner will be announced, but if they want to put an excerpt on the Web site by Dec. 21 and have time for formatting and final editing, then I'm guessing it will be 4 to 6 weeks from now. Maybe a mention that *Adrift* was a semi-finalist in the contest will help.

Here's the contest announcement:

From the Editor of Anderbo: Kate, your 2011 Anderbo No-Fee Novel Contest entry is one of 8 Semi-Finalists. (There were over 450 entries.) We'd like to see the next 9,000 words of your manuscript—no attachments, please; just in the body of the email.

Sincerely,

Rick Rofihe

http://www.anderbo.com/

The Mercer Street Books Fiction Prize

Anderbo.com wishes to post up to the first 36 manuscript pages of an unpublished novel on its Web site by December 21st, 2011 for at least the following six months. We will look at the FIRST 36 PAGES (up to 9,000 words) of your e-manuscript submitted to editors@anderbo.com and decide within 60 days of its arrival if we want to see more.

From: Tom
Sent: Wednesday, September 28, 2011, 8:49 AM
Subject: Congratulations

That looks like wonderful recognition and an excellent lever for marketing. Good luck in the finals.

From: Tom
Sent: Wednesday, September 28, 2011, 12:38 PM
Subject: My Edits

Here are the most recent chapters (Chapters 11 to 15). There are some nice images here. I'm still confused about the timing of everything—see note on last page.[1]

Notes:

1. Tom's two notes at the end of Chapter 15:

A. You use "OK" a lot. This is not a bad thing, but it's sometimes jarring to see it as two letters. In colloquial speech, we usually see "okay." [Associated Press Stylebook lists preferred usage as OK. Usage stands in final *Adrift* text.]

B. Okay, now I'm getting really confused. I thought Lizette went to her father's (opening scene of book) after her stay in the hospital. Then she went to Sandy's and the Dog House to hang out. She got into cleaning and then got weird, annoyed the Dogs, and Rocket abandoned her downtown. Then when it got cold she crept back into the basement (I'm working from memory here, not checking back through the chapters) and watched Cadillac Carl kill a druggie. After that she fled to the island and Marian, Poland, and Abaya—where we've been for about ten chapters.

So … when did the attack happen? We saw it in a dream after she got to the island. Was there an attack in the alley after Rocket dropped her downtown? Or was it before she went to the hospital, got violent, went to the psycho ward, was released by Dr. Finch, and then went to see her father? And if she was attacked and went to the hospital after Rocket dropped her, when did she get out?

Lizette's head may be filled with spaghetti because of her sickness. Maybe the reader should be all confused about time and place and event, too, in order to share her confusion. But since we're sharing other viewpoints as well, not just Lizette's, this all seems like just sloppy coordination.

From: Kate
Sent: Thursday, September 29, 2011, 6:24 AM
Subject: Fighting Fire

Dear Tom:

I've read your edits and comments twice in preparation for making changes to the manuscript this weekend. Your thoughtful comments, catches, and logic are so helpful that all I can say is "thanks." Working with an accomplished novelist/editor is incredibly valuable, in that you keep the story—beginning to end, detail by detail—in your head and follow the narrative under the layers to keep the storyline tight and the fabric gathered.

At least a dozen readers have gone through the manuscript, but haven't noted the logic faults and confused details that you rightly point out. I'm amazed and grateful that at Chapter 15, you're sending me back to Chapter 1 because you remember and want a detail checked! That is a great gift to me. As I'm learning to be a novelist, keeping everything in the narrative in my head is a challenge.

When you read the first chapters you said the writing was like a blast from a fire hose. I like that way of telling this story, but I also understand that control of the spew is essential—for me and for the reader—and you're helping me get a grip on the nozzle. I can't wait to get to work on this new section from you. Thanks again.

From: Kate
Sent: Sunday, October 2, 2011, 3:02 PM
Subject: Making Things Richer

Hi Elizabeth and Tom:

First—Congratulations, Elizabeth, on the launch of *Wanting to be Jackie Kennedy.* I'm knocked out by the quality of the book, by your actions to get it into the hands of readers, by your great example. I'm sincerely thrilled for you and inspired. Can't wait to see what happens next.

And, thank you again, Tom, for your support and outstanding expertise as an editor. What I value most is that you understand what I'm trying to do, apply discipline, but don't intrude on the creative expression. Instead, you open up ways to make the story richer. I don't want to be effusive in my thanks and undermine the sincerity, but I really mean it.

I just received the notice below about the Mercer Street Book Award. I have not yet, as requested, sent the next 9,000 words, which Tom and I have already revised. I want to look at it again before firing it off. I've looked at the http://www.anderbo.com/ Web site and think it is an online community in the literary vein that I've been working toward. The literary fiction niche is narrow and cliquey. Sometimes these kinds of books cross over to mainstream, sometimes not. I've read that it's one of the hardest markets to crack and I'm afraid to hope. But there you are.

You are one of 4 Finalists in the 2011 Anderbo No-Fee Novelist Contest; please send us the next 9,000 words of your novel-manuscript in the body of an email. Based on the first up to 27,000 words you've submitted, we'll either ask to see the balance of your novel, OR list your entry on the Contest page as one of the Top 4 entries, based on however many words of your novel-manuscript we've seen. In any case, keep in mind that while there will probably be only one winner, your entry is already in the top 1% of the over 450 entries, and that that in itself is an accomplishment. Sincerely, The Editors of Anderbo

––––––––––

From: Tom
Sent: Monday, October 3, 2011, 11:22 AM
Subject: Congratulations on Top 4 Placement, and Best of
  Luck on Being the Final-Finalist

Some thoughts on your final paragraph, about "crossing over to mainstream" and "hardest markets to crack." Now that the combination of ereader devices and internet distribution and marketing have virtually put a stop to the Gutenberg Revolution and launched the reading world into a new age— and that practically overnight, a lot faster than Gutenberg's printed Bibles ever caught on—we have to reexamine our definitions and expectations as writers.

I really believe that the "eye of the needle" that press runs and publishing costs have put us through has distorted our mission as storytellers. Marketing has thrown up category after category, and authors have tried to fit their work into the latest and most profitable trends. One of (scientist and bestselling sci-fi author) David Brin's postings on Facebook showed a flowchart of 100 top science fiction novels and how they fit into various sub-genres like "dystopian," "cyber punk," and "humanist."

Then other authors in their comments on that posting began quarreling over the fit of the definitions, such as whether Heinlein was a real humanist because he kept using deus-ex-machinae like the Archangel Michael in *Stranger in a Strange Land* and Mycroft the Computer in *Moon is a Harsh Mistress.*

I can remember as a lad when science fiction was one genre, while "mystery" and "romance" were others. All the rest of the books were some undefined shade of mainstream, throwing together the naval adventures of C.S. Forester and the historical romances of John Fowles and Thomas B. Costain, with no separate classification. And at the middle of the last century, mainstream fiction actually was considered "literary fiction."

My response to Brin's posting was: For reasons I can't fully express, breaking up the book world into neat and convenient genres and sub-genres deeply depresses me. It's like editors, agents, and readers are telling me, "You can't really think up anything new. Your work is just part of a trend already established by a dozen or a hundred other writers. Go sit on aisle four, shelf two, with the rest of your kind." Every book should come with its own surprises. We're in the business of making handheld universes here, not grinding out link sausages!

One reason I stopped trying to send manuscripts to prospective agents, aside from the largely negative return on effort, was reading all those sub-genres in *The Literary Marketplace.* When Danielle Steele and her sisters get a whole genre called "glitz," I just want to give up and go home.

I think, I hope, I greatly desire, that the new outpouring of writing in the Digital Revolution, will crack all this genre mania apart like a badly flawed crystal. Readers at first will be dismayed at finding a "loss of quality" in self-published books, but there are a lot of traditionally published books today filled with factual, grammatical, and typographical errors. (Posters are already noting and addressing this on LinkedIn's The Writers' Network. The best comment was, "Cream will rise to the top.")

Readers may also feel some loss at not having publishers steer authors into accepted sub-genres, but that will quickly pass. William Gibson gave us the first cyber punk novel in the mid-'80s, and it was immediately picked up and valued as something unique and new. Tom Clancy gave us techno-thrillers and had a great success (and it was a near-run thing that he didn't end up in science fiction). Danielle Steele did the same for glitz. Stephen King single-handedly revived American horror.

Each of these unique authors was followed by dozens or hundreds of others, all at the suggestion of their agents and editors. But now there's no need for the rest of us to chase the success of a few trailblazers. There will be no "collective wisdom" of agents and editors deciding that any work is too limited in marketing potential to be rewarded with a publishing contract.

Sure, some writers will watch the market and try to cash in on some other writer's success. But the book market will soon be going in a thousand different directions all at once. Right after the success of Gibson's *Neuromancer,* there was a fine line between writing a cyber punk novel and simply aping the world view, technological vision, and writing style of William Gibson. A lot of people got away with it because editors and agents were hungry to follow a proven success in the market. In the Digital Revolution, that's going to be known for what it is: copycatting.

My point is that the world has turned upside down. Success isn't going to be built on your book's finding, copying, or happening to fall into some magic formula for success, appealing to a mega-audience, breaking into the mainstream, and hitting it big. There is no "mass mind" out there waiting for the perfect book. There may be currents of interest based on the zeitgeist, or current affairs, or political and technological trends and events—but they're going to be transitory.

Those of us who write for the long-term have to go for the human heart, human curiosity, and the human hunger to be told a story. It won't matter whether a book fits the techno-thriller category or the science fiction category. Does it delight and intrigue the reader? If so, it will find an audience. The age of the bestseller—with waves of success mania sweeping the book marketplace—may well be over. That's going to be bad news for the one-tenth of one percent of authors who in the past have made a huge success. It's going to be great news for the rest of us who will find the readers our books deserve.

So keep writing your book, and make it the very best of your own particular thing that it can be. That's going to be success in the new age. It will be a smaller success, but the delighted reader, who finds something that resonates with his or her personal taste and is willing to give word-of-mouth appreciation, is the most loyal. It will take time, but with ebooks time is on our side. And we're all around for the long haul.

P.S. I just looked into your email with the link to Meghan Ward on self-publishing.[1] A lot of good advice. I don't see anything that conflicts with what I say above.

P.P.S. I got a payment notice from Amazon a week ago. While royalties in August were a mere $12, in September they more than doubled to $27. If this trend continues, I'll be a millionaire by Christmas 2012—and own all the stars in the galaxy by the Christmas after that! Whoo-ee!

Notes:

1. Meghan Ward, writer and book editor (http://www.meghanward.com/editing.html), recently completed a memoir titled *Paris On Less Than $10,000 a Day.*

From: Kate
Date: Thursday, October 6, 2011, 5:30 AM
Subject: Getting a Grip

Dear Tom:

Here's the next installment of *Adrift,* about 12,000 words (Chapters 16 to 20). I've gone over the chapters carefully, trying to cut down on the work for you, feeling more confident about what needs to be fixed based on your previous editing. I hope the work reflects your tutelage. It has been hard to concentrate this week as I wait for the decision on the Mercer Street Book Award. The editors called for the full manuscript, which I sent. They had previously only seen the manuscript up to the chapters we'd already worked on. Cha. 16 to 20 were messy—clumsy stage direction, dialog confusion, extraneous information. I'm afraid to think about the rest of the story, what the editors will think. Crap! No way will *Adrift* win.

But, the good news is that I'm getting a better handle on the revision process, with your help, and *Adrift* is going to be a much tighter, better book when we're done. Thanks for that. I've been working on this section since 2:30 AM and have a 10-hour workday ahead of me. I greatly appreciate your comments on the artificial boundaries of genre and how that has constrained the delivery of good stories to readers, what a disservice the marketing system has been for everyone—authors, readers, publishers. Your comments are thought provoking and I'd like to hear more from you on this subject. You've been in the publishing trenches for a long time and you're a keen observer. I don't have the energy to respond intelligently at the moment.

As always, thanks for your help. Please send an update on how your own projects are going when you have a chance. I heard a story about an amazing breakthrough in stem cell research on NPR yesterday, made me think about the story you talked about—the visionary leader with the ability to continue on while those around him fell along the way. The death of Steve Jobs also made me think about the story you outlined. Whatever you're working on, I wish you the best.

From: Tom
Sent: Friday, October 14, 2011, 5:35 PM
Subject: Chapters 16-20

Here are my edits and comments. Overall, this seems much smoother and more controlled than earlier chapters. I'm still not sure where the story's going, though.

Sorry to be so long with this, but I've had a spot of illness and am wrestling with my own book. I've got the Methuselah book on hold as it is too soon to do yet. I've been working on a book about aliens and time travel. Hope to have something by the end of the year, but I have to get the incidents and connections right. Everything depends on internal logic.

From: Kate
Sent: Saturday, October 15, 2011, 6:52 AM
Subject: Building a Battleship

Dear Tom:

Sorry to hear you've been under the weather and hope you're feeling better. I'd appreciate an update on your current project and will gladly provide feedback when you're done, if that would help to you. Your *Adrift* edits arrived in time for me to work on them this weekend, which is perfect. Great catches! The over-laden arc welding simile, clumsy staging in the dump, etc.

And, thanks for catching Lizette taking Violet's birth certificate. I want to keep the action small, but it's important in that it shows her intent, albeit subconscious, in advance of future story developments. The book totals 34 chapters, so we're past the halfway mark, Greg's death and Violet's birth serving as the story's apex. The novel's pace picks up now and starts galloping for home. As to where that is, the end point, I'm reluctant to say because I need your fresh eyes to check if the denouement works.

Points of fact: Ambulance drivers and attendants in the late 1960s-early 1970s didn't have the skill level of today's paramedics. In 1966, the National Academy of Sciences and the American Medical Association described an appalling picture of emergency care in the United States and gave critical attention to the standards of ambulances and ambulance attendants in their report entitled "Accidental Death and Disability: The Neglected Disease of Modern Society."

There were no generally accepted standards for training or competence for ambulance personnel or specifications for ambulance transport vehicles until the Emergency Medical Service (EMS) System Act, passed into law in 1973. Further, the then popular Cadillac station wagon-type ambulances were found to be unsuitable for treating patients in transit. More than 50% of the country's ambulance services before 1973 were provided by morticians. The hearse driver/funeral director also doubled as the ambulance driver/ambulance attendant in most rural areas.

Adrift in the Sound is set in 1973, and much of the story takes place in rural Washington, before the standards and advanced training requirements we expect from emergency services today were implemented. The guys who met Marian and Greg at the ferry dock in Anacortes where meat wagon drivers in an old hearse. Also, midwives weren't licensed to practice in Washington State until 1975, one of the nation's first states to officially recognize the profession. Although views on midwifery were changing in 1973, the practice was not, strictly speaking, legal. Marian, who has a B.S. and R.N. from the University of Washington, trained at the Frontier Nursing Service in Kentucky, which was founded in 1925 and was the nation's first organization to use nurses trained as midwives. They traveled on horseback to remote areas in the Appalachians to assist women with childbirth and provide basic medical care to poor families.

Do you think these details need to be worked back into the story for the reader's sake? I'm reluctant to over-burden the narrative with this information. While writing *Adrift,* I had a problem with Marian taking over the story and had to strip back the narrative in a number of places to hold Lizette in higher relief as the main character. I had a whole chapter on Marian and Greg in the ER, providing an explanation for her decision to head for Harbor View Hospital, where she had worked for a while as a trauma nurse. Adair Lara advised taking the chapter out, reasoning that it detracted from

Lizette's story as the main character. Lizette has been an interesting character to work with because she is so passive-aggressive, easily overshadowed by other characters and the action. Adair's concern is that I not let Lizette sink below the reader's radar.

As I told you when we met at Elizabeth's, my intention with *Adrift in the Sound* is to present an engaging story set in a moment of horrendous social/political change. Changes we're still dealing with today. The story takes place in the farthest reach of America, while ripples of change were expanding in all directions across America, swamping many who were still stuck in the free-love '60s Cultural Revolution. As I've said, not everybody survived.

From the end of *Adrift* Chapter 20:

"A fish leapt in Lake Union, spreading concentric circles that changed the shape of the world, but no one noticed."

My intention with *Adrift* is to create both art and artifact, while telling an engaging story from a woman's perspective that the average reader will enjoy. At the same time, without the reader noticing, I hope, I've built a social history battleship with a deep interpretative draft that will withstand enemy fire. You are helping make sure it's seaworthy and I am grateful for that.

Here's a glimpse of the stealth I'm aiming for: http://katecampbell.blogspot.com/2011/06/fighting-and-winning-at-midway.html. Thanks.

From: Tom
Sent: Sunday, October 16, 2011, 11:17 AM
Subject: Driving a Team of Wild Horses

I think I understand what you're trying to do. But if you don't provide the reader some context—like the state of emergency medical services at the time of your story—most readers will just blow right by and insert images of what they know from today. Think, for example, if one of your characters needed an abortion, you'd have to explain why she didn't just bop down to the women's clinic and get one. It would be a complicated and illicit affair, and you'd need some mental dialog about a woman's most basic, life-changing situation not being addressed in a realistic fashion.

I'm a baby-boomer who was three years out of college by 1973, but I still didn't recall anything about what ambulances might have looked like back then. Most of your readers under 50 won't remember 1973 very well, if at all. Even if a reader was born by then, most people under age 12 aren't aware of facts in the bigger world around them. If you want to make a mosaic of the world as it existed then, you must make these different circumstances stand out.

In this context, maybe it would be appropriate if you provided a "Reader's Guide" at the end of the book addressing each of these issues. (Reading clubs like to have the extra information.) Rather than a chronology of events, it would address situations in the world of 1973 pertinent to your story in language just like your paragraphs below. Some suggestions: Roe v. Wade (and why Sandy didn't get an abortion in the first place), quasi-legal status of midwifery, ambulance and emergency services, involuntary mental health treatment, psychotropic medications and their side effects. But having such an appendix still does not relieve you of making the current situation clear in the text of the book. You just wouldn't have to provide chapter and verse in the text about pending legislation and such.

So, at the point when they meet the ambulance at the ferry dock, someone—probably Marian, because I think she's POV at that point—has to internally comment that it looks like a hearse painted red and white, and the drivers are standing around like hearse drivers instead of helping her like medical professionals. Inside, Marian finds only the most primitive medical supplies—essentially a first-aid kit. In her moment of emergency with Greg, she can imagine something better: an attendant with medical training and a kit with some basic tools like a blood-pressure cuff and oxygen. You can put Lizette inside with her, so that Marian can explain some of this and her wish for a better-equipped medical world to your main character. This can all be handled with a paragraph or two, and make your point about a world needing change.

This appreciation of the medical situation would also go a long way to explaining Greg's death. When Marian first suggests Harbor View in Seattle, let her mention that she knew their facility best—it would also help if we knew she was a former trauma nurse, and not just a country midwife. (You may have said that somewhere earlier in the book, but it needs to be emphasized here again, to make her choice of a distant hospital clear.) Again, this is easy with a sentence or two. But now, faced with an 80-mile trip in a converted hearse without proper supplies, let her have second thoughts. Yet she doesn't know where else to go! This puts pressure on your story and prepares us for the news that Greg didn't make it. And, again, you can have some of this through Lizette's eyes: seeing her friend worry and grieve over the decisions about an emergency that Marian in fact caused with the hubcap, defending Lizette herself. This can help Lizette focus and become a bit more adult in the process.

One thing in the last chapter. If midwifery is only quasi-legal, does Marian have power to issue and sign a birth certificate? Perhaps her R.N. status needs to be re-inserted here to justify it. And if she has official capacity, would she issue a fill-in-the-blanks document that the parents might later falsify in some way (as we intuit Lizette might)? You need to have her explain to Sandy that she's leaving the baby's name blank because Sandy hasn't picked one yet, and that the parent names are blank because then Sandy gets to name the father. Marian might explain this offhandedly to Lizette. And that would explain how Lizette appreciates the value—to herself, later—of possessing a blank but signed birth certificate. Now, as to why it's undated, you'll have to think of a reason. ...

You're driving a team with a lot of horses here: what's happening in the story, why 1973 is a time of needed change, what's happening inside Lizette's head. Driving them gracefully and dropping just the right hints and messages are all part of the art that we've chosen. You're doing pretty well with this, but I'm a bit concerned. You're reacting to various previous readers—you mention Adair Lara—by simply cutting out whole chapters. When you do that, you need to examine and note elements needed to push the story forward, then work them back into the parts that remain. More effing structural work.

It's really quite amazing, when you think about it. We all start with a blank sheet of paper—or an empty computer screen—and end up with such complicated lives-that-never-were unfolding out of nothing but our imaginations.

From: Kate
Sent: Sunday, October 16, 2011, 4:12 PM
Subject: Author Toni Morrison and the Role of a Good Editor

Dear Tom:

I'm reading *Paradise,* the novel by Nobel Laureate Toni Morrison, which is an astonishing display of craftsmanship, among other wonderful things. Because her work is brilliant and I haven't read her before, I looked for interviews online to learn more about her.

I was curious about how long it took her to write the book. In an interview in the *Paris Review* she said her books take at least three years to complete, which made me feel better about how long *Adrift* is taking me to finish. She also talked about the difference between dithering with a manuscript and making substantive revisions. Before you agreed to help me, I think I was just dithering, not recognizing the problems and where revisions were actually needed. I was caught up in copy editing the manuscript to death, putting in, taking out, putting back in. *Adrift,* so to speak.

Morrison said this about editing and her editor Robert Gottlieb, who also edited John Cheever, John le Carre, Ray Bradbury, Elia Kazan, and Michael Crichton and served as editor of *The New Yorker* from 1987 to 1992: "I had a very good editor, superlative for me—Bob Gottlieb. What made him good for me was a number of things—knowing what not to touch; asking all the questions you probably would have asked yourself had there been the time.

"Good editors are really the third eye. Cool. Dispassionate. They don't love you or your work; for me that is what is valuable—not compliments. Sometimes it's uncanny; the editor puts his or her finger on exactly the place the writer knows is weak but just couldn't do any better at the time. Or perhaps the writer thought it might fly, but wasn't sure.

"Good editors identify that place and sometimes make suggestions. Some suggestions are not useful because you can't explain everything to an editor about what you are trying to do. I couldn't possibly explain all of those things to an editor, because what I do has to work on so many levels. But within the relationship, if there is some trust, some willingness to listen, remarkable things can happen."

I do not suggest in any way that my feeble efforts approach a writer of Morrison's stature, but I believe you are a very good editor for me and I trust you. And, crap! I stripped out too much Marian-related story and will have to go back and piece things in. Adair didn't suggest either/or. She suggested that Marian was overshadowing Lizette in places and perhaps I should look at dialing her back. I used an ax when a scalpel might have been a better tool. I should have fought for the deleted chapter, found ways to work some of the material into different places, but didn't have confidence about things that needed to stay or go, sought and got too much advice from too many sources—making changes, changing things back, wanting the story to be good, but not really knowing how to do it and, worst of all, I didn't stand up for my work. I want to be acquiescent, open to criticism, not defensive, willing to listen and find ways to make the story stronger. But there comes a point when the author has to say NO! to editing changes. I don't know when to stand up!

I just went back to Chapter 6 where the reader first meets Marian and she prepares a bath for Lizette. There's mention of her diplomas and midwife certificate in the bathroom. I slipped it by you, but you found me out, thought maybe slowing down for the details wasn't necessary for the reader. But, she could not have gotten a midwife's certificate in Washington State at that time, which I think the text implies—it wasn't legal and there were no training schools there, although public health officials were well aware that it was going on, hence the debate at the time. Her certificate is from the Frontier Nursing Service in Kentucky.

But, that is not the case today. I have been in correspondence with friends who founded the state's first home birth program in Washington, which is going strong today and is now affiliated with the University of Washington and its teaching hospital. I will have to check with them to confirm when/ if midwives could officially sign birth certificates. They certainly couldn't in 1973 in Washington, but they could in Kentucky, which is why Marian didn't give signing it much thought. She'd previously done it all the time.

Also, regardless of state law, women in the region's large Scandinavian community preferred home births, which was/ is common in Europe. Physicians in Washington often signed the document post delivery, after well-baby checks. Marian wanted to provide the option of proof and was fully aware of the debate about licensing for midwives that was going on at the time in Washington. It was legalized in November 1975, effective January 1976, and my son Mark was delivered by midwives at home in Seattle on February 7, 1976, among the first legal home deliveries by midwives in the state, but his birth certificate is signed by a supervising physician, a guy who stopped by the house after the fact to make sure there were no problems.

I worked as an advocate for home births while I lived in Seattle. Sandy's birth story in *Adrift* is a lightly fictionalized version of my own birth story, which I wrote a few days after Mark was born and have carried it around with me ever since, now crafting it into the story. And, from my connection with the women's health collective, I also was acutely aware of the atrocities that occurred because abortion wasn't legal, which I won't go into. Bottom line—in 1973, the legal status of practicing midwifery and attending at home births was nebulous. Unless something went horribly wrong with a birth, Marian was not likely to be arrested. Arrests did occur in other states around this time period, however. This is too much information, I apologize.

What I mean to say is this: You've raised excellent points, made constructive suggestions, and the information needs to be folded into the narrative creatively and minimally to maintain the narrative flow and buoy the story. It will take me some time to do this work, but I agree it's essential.

Your comment about driving a lot of horses made me think about my father. When I was a child we lived on my grandmother's ranch in west Marin County and my father, an accomplished horseman and trainer, ran the stable in Lagunitas. In the fall, we'd go into San Francisco for the Grand National Rodeo at the Cow Palace where my father often worked as a wrangler. One year the Budweiser Clydesdale horses performed, pulling the beer wagon at break-neck speed around the arena, figure eights, crisscrosses, the horses flying, spotlights barely keeping up. The regular driver got hurt and my father drove the team for the remaining performances.

I remember huge, beautiful horses, each weighing about a ton, perfectly color matched, and spotlighted in shiny harnesses. My father drove the team, eight-in-hand, directing them with just the lift of his fingers against the gathered reins. The performance was precise and mesmerizing. I want to write like that.

You are a very good editor for me and I'm lucky to work with you. Thanks for looking out for the reader, putting your finger on weak places, and not letting my horses get away from me.

From: Tom
Sent: Sunday, October 16, 2011, 8:59 PM
Subject: Thanks

Thanks for the appreciation. I wonder if Toni's Robert Gottlieb is the same person who runs the Trident Media Agency and is Pat Larkin's agent?

From: Kate
Sent: Monday, October 17, 2011, 5:07 AM
Subject: Not to Be Confused

Hi Tom:

No, it's not the same person. Pat's Robert Gottlieb started Trident Media Group, LLC in September 2000 after working as an agent for 24 years at the William Morris Agency. He now serves as chairman and serves as agent for many best-selling authors including Tom Clancy, Dean Koontz, and Janet Evanovich, to name a few. He continues to grow his list of authors which currently include international best-selling authors Deepak Chopra, Catherine Coulter, Elizabeth George, Sherrilyn Kenyon, Kat Martin, Mary Alice Monroe, and Karen Robards.

Toni Morrison's Gottlieb is now in his 80's and much more a literary editor, rather than an agent. Robert Gottlieb began his career in 1955 as an editorial assistant at Simon & Schuster. Later, he was publisher and editor in chief of Alfred A. Knopf and, for five years, the editor in chief of *The New Yorker* magazine. Gottlieb discovered Joseph Heller's *Catch 22,* and while working at Knopf he encouraged Toni Morrison to quit her job as an editor there and become a full-time novelist.

Bill Clinton requested Gottlieb when it came time to write his own memoirs, and Gottlieb also worked on the autobiographies of celebrities like Lauren Bacall, Sidney Poitier, John Lennon, and Bob Dylan. The literary works he has edited include those by Ray Bradbury, Salman Rushdie, John Cheever, and V. S. Naipaul. In other words, like you, Gottlieb knows his stuff.

I'm off on story assignment for a few days—San Diego and Riverside counties. Will get back to work on *Adrift* next weekend. Hate to slow down, but need to do my job and put bread on the table, the story of my life. Talk to you soon.

P.S. Attached is the next batch of chapters—about 13,000 words, 4 chapters (Chapters 21 to 24). The manuscript includes 34 chapters, so we're making great progress, two more batches after this one and we're done! Sincere thanks for your help. Look forward to your response.

From: Tom
Sent: Friday, October 28, 2011, 12:47 PM
Subject: No Fuss

Here are my edits and comments on the recent chapters. I am finding less and less to fuss with—which is either a good thing, because you are self-editing ahead of me, or a bad thing, because I'm getting lulled by familiarity with your style and not paying so much attention. Either way, the story seems to be picking up.

One note: I forget whether in the early chapters you were using the serial comma or not, but you are definitely not using it in these recent chapter sets. You should really use it or not consistently—something to check and change in the final pass.

From: Kate
Sent: Friday, October 28, 2011, 1:37 PM
Subject: Doing It with Style

Hi Tom:

Thanks so much for the new edited batch of chapters and for your observation that things seem cleaner. I think you're as watchful and precise as ever with your editing. But I edited the last batches of chapters before sending them to you, putting to use what I'd learned from you in earlier chapters and I also think my writing improved as I wrote the later chapters. I had a lot of trouble getting the opening chapters to work and sorely needed your help to straighten out the mess I'd created.

I'm glad you've brought up the issue of serial comma. Because I write to Associated Press Style, *Adrift* is written that way. I have chosen not to use semicolons in the manuscript, because I feel the construction is too sophisticated for the content and style of this story. If a semicolon is absolutely needed, then the sentence(s) need to be recast. AP Style is sans comma before serial conjunction.

I have concern, however, about the need to use proper literary manuscript style in direct and indirect quotation. *Chicago*

Manual of Style for this? I don't know if you got to the place where Poland tells the story of the spoiled girl and the Bear Clan, but I worried about the use of quotes within quotes within quotes and trusted you'd tell me if style and usage were wrong. I believe the Chicago Manual would be the source for the correct punctuation in this matter. I will look at the section in *Adrift* again. I've looked at it a couple of times and it seems right, but don't trust my judgment. I'd feel better if I had a grasp of Chicago Style.

But I would make the case for using AP Style in a literary manuscript, this one anyway, because it is written in a very mainstream and informal style that is reader friendly, the intention of newspapers, and because it is habitual to me and my personal writing style after 40 years of use. You, of the dozen or so people who've read the manuscript and commented, are the only one to bring up the use of punctuation style, which has been a worry to me. Your noticing style is another reason, I'm grateful for your help.

I'm looking forward to digging into your edits. I always learn a lot from your work. Thanks again.

From: Tom
Sent: Friday, October 28, 2011, 2:43 PM
Subject: Perils of Punctuation

Kate—

I was trained in *Chicago Manual* as a university press editor (and actually was given a week-long seminar with the then-current editors of the manual in 1970). I've also used U.S. Government Printing Office (no serial comma) and AP (ditto). I personally stick with the serial comma because it's simply clearer. In your book, where you often use a lot of serials without a final conjunction (made-up example: "she was drifting, falling, turning, tumbling to her death") it looks kind of funny not to continue the rhythm of the commas if you stick in the conjunction ("she was drifting, falling, turning and tumbling to her death") because it makes turning and tumbling seem like a separate group of activities from the drifting and falling.

In any event, readers of any kind of writing—journalism, science fiction, literary fiction, cereal box ingredient labels—will have come to accept either style. Most won't even notice if you drift between one style and the other. But for those who do notice, it will BUG THE HELL OUT OF THEM. Books have been thrown across the room with great force because of drifting style. If you're comfortable with AP and no serial comma, then by all means continue it. (And if I edited in some serial commas earlier on, and haven't done it now, then shame on me, and please do your best to fix my errors.)

As to the quotes, I remember Poland telling one story from his culture and didn't notice any confusion of quotes. Generally, I follow the tack that if the character is speaking a text from some other source, I try to put the quote inside single quote marks, where the speaking is in double quotes. If the character is quoting a text with spoken quotes within it, then those internal quotes get double quotes again.

"Look," Peewee said, "I'm not going up on the high diving board ever again. To take a leaf from Mr. Poe's book, 'Quoth the raven, "Nevermore!" ' "

Note that in the facetious example above, we end up with three sets of quotes, double-single-double, without a break. I've shown them spaced out for clarity, but most writers would just pile them on. When you get to either paper printing or ebook text, this has the unfortunate tendency to look like five little hooky things in a row. Unfortunately, if you space them out for clarity as I've done here, they won't stick together (and Word will also autocorrect the second and third into open quotes rather than closed). If this little train of punctuation marks falls right at the end of a line (which can happen in any ebook format where the reader has control of type size) then they might break awkwardly to the next line. I solve this by adding a Word Symbol, the nonbreaking space, between the spaced out quotes. In the ebook, this gets replaced by the HTML code   which does the same thing. (Similar problems befall spaced periods trying to form an ellipsis, which is why I use the HTML … code.)

And yes, the acronym OCD does mean something to me. Next time …

From: Kate
Sent: Thursday, November 3, 2011, 8:15 PM
Subject: Chapters 25 to 28

Hi Tom:

Attached is the next batch of Chapters for *Adrift*. There was a delay in getting them to you because my hard drive crashed and I had to buy a new computer and get the data transferred. I've searched for nearly three hours and can't find the master *Adrift* file that has all the latest revisions on the new system. I'll call and find out where my most current files are stored on the new system. Or I may have to take the computer system back to the tech and get him to show me where they are stored. Because of my work schedule, it could be another week before everything is straightened out.

But I'm only mildly hysterical since I stored all revisions to the master manuscript through Chapter 11 on a thumb drive as backup. The attached chapters may not be as clean as the version I can't find on my new system right now, but they're close. I need to remain calm, keep working on the manuscript, and not lose momentum. I'll see if I can recover the most current files or find out where they are hidden, but may have to go back to Chapter 12 and begin revising again from there. In the meantime, here's the next batch.

I don't know what your workload is right now. I'm afraid to ask. Let me know what you're up to when you have a chance. Thanks for your patience and kindness.

From: Tom
Sent: Friday, November 4, 2011, 11:24:43 AM
Subject: Re: Adrift Chapters 25 to 28

Kate—

What an awful thing to have happen! I hope you recover everything. Since our pair of little earthquakes in Berkeley a couple of weeks ago, I've started diligently backing up daily work from important folders (your book is one of them) on a stand-alone hard drive on my desk—where I can grab it, rip out the cords, and run.

I'll start working on these chapters, but I can't promise to have them for you much before the middle of the month. Irene and I are flying to Austin to visit Pat Larkin and family next week. Short visit—just a long weekend—but I'm scrambling to bring the Jongleur time-travel book to a stopping place before we leave. I have 60,000 pretty solid words on a projected 60-70,000, so I should be done before the end of the year.

Good luck with the techno-end.

From: Kate
Sent: Saturday, November 5, 2011, 10:10 AM
Subject: Playing the Puck

Dear Tom:

Thanks for the update on your progress. Can't wait to read your time traveler book! And, going to see Pat in Texas sounds like great fun, although my colonial view of Texas is tumbleweeds and obnoxious men behaving badly. I hope he's doing well and that you'll give him my regards, compliment him on his cowboy hat.

I'm the pot on the electric burner with the water boiled dry. Smoke alarm hasn't gone off yet. This morning it's yoga with an intense teacher. That should guarantee leg cramps. Then a nap. Don't worry about Chapters 25 to 28. I'm still working out the computer glitches. The tech downloaded my old data just fine. It was in a recovery file from the previous computer's crash. Now I need to take the new computer back in and get him to download the most recent work. That's what he missed. Duh!

It will probably be another week before my system is fully restored. In the meantime, I'm loving my new system! Like hockey star Wayne Gretzky, I'm going to play where the puck is going to be, not where it's at. I'm going to try not grousing over the unexpected expense, trusting that everything will turn out OK. I have most of the revised manuscript and your editing in hard copy. You are a great teammate. Gretzky should be so lucky. Thanks.

From: Tom
Sent: Tuesday, November 8, 2011, 5:36 PM
Subject: Slicing and Dicing

Kate—

Here are my edits and comments on the most recent chapters. (I got done with my other work a little ahead of the Austin trip.) This is beginning to come together now, at least as far as I can see. Less "slice of life" and more story. Still don't know how sensible Lizette is, but if she ever gets the painting ownership straightened out with the gallery, she's rich for 1973.

From: Kate
Sent: Wednesday, November 9, 2011, 3:32 AM
Subject: Beans and Barbecue

Dear Tom:

You are a Prince! Perfect timing with this batch of chapters. Yesterday went back to the computer tech and stood there while he downloaded ALL files from old computer to the new system, which I love—faster and cleaner operation. Don't know how he missed them, something about four unique addresses on one computer, a configuration he'd never seen before, therefore confusing him.

I have the master *Adrift* manuscript safely back on board. Now to work on the two chapter batches from you. I'm grateful that you'll be in Texas, eating beans and barbecue while I catch up with my revisions. There are only four chapters left to revise, three months of work so far.

Maybe I'm getting ahead of myself, but I see the next step as reading the entire manuscript for flow and the errant typo. Then conversion to type. I'd like to have galleys because sometimes in the typeset form the eye catches things it didn't see before. Don't know if Elizabeth's process allows for this, but I want to see proof pages. I meet with her on the 19th to discuss publishing *Adrift* through her imprint and will ask about the process of finalizing. Do you have any suggestions about the process of putting finishing touches on the manuscript and preparing to print? What procedures do you follow to get your manuscripts into as perfect a condition as possible?

I hope you and Irene have a great trip and that you'll share photos and details when you get back. Thanks for your help. I'll be splashing around in the Sound until you get back.

From: Tom
Sent: Wednesday, November 9, 2011, 10:31 AM
Subject: Shade Tree Mechanics

Kate—

Since any process of converting your manuscript to galleys—or more likely page proofs with some layout program like InDesign or Framemaker—will start with your Word document, you want that to reflect everything in the final book. This means, first, a close final read. You want to turn on the paragraph marks (button with the para symbol on your toolbar) and make sure all the paragraphs are properly indented. Either all formatted as indented or tabbed as indented (not a mix, as I've seen in some of the chapters I'm reading). Then do a find/replace on extra spaces. I've taken them out where spotted, but you want to do this mechanically, too. Word doesn't show up extra spaces as much of a problem, but they create funny gaps in printed matter. Finally, you want to consider how you handle things like dashes (space-Word en-dash-space, or nospace-emdash-nospace, which is preferred) and those single/double quote clusters (in the last chapters I put in a non-breaking space—shows up in paragraph marks as a dot with a blue tilde).

When I do all this, it's with HTML coding in mind. I don't deal with the printed word anymore, as we've discussed. HTML actually makes things simpler, because you add coding for every piece of punctuation or symbol not in the basic ASCII set. All smart quotes, dashes, ellipses, diacritics, and special symbols like ampersands and copyrights have their own code, which I find/replace successively.

You will want to take a book, like one of Elizabeth's, and work up a copyright page. She and her designer will have ideas, but think about your claims and disclaimers, like the "any similarity to persons living or dead ..." stuff.

You also want to think about your chapter headings and cover. You were talking about woodcuts of the Native American symbols. Since the orca plays such a dominant role in the book, you might want to go online and check Getty Images and other photo sources. You can buy a "royalty free" (that is, nonexclusive use) image of about a megabyte for a couple of hundred dollars. I collect about a dozen in my Getty lightbox, go back and noodle them, and then pick one. (You'll be doing it with the help of Elizabeth's designer.)

You probably want to get the actual copyright done with the page proofs or the final book. But be sure to go online with the Library of Congress and get it squared away.

Elizabeth, who's gone through all this with her Jackie Kennedy book, will be a good source of advice. I'll be in touch next week.

From: Kate
Sent: Wednesday, November 9, 2011, 11:35 AM
Subject: Happy Trails

You just told me exactly what I wanted to know! Talk to you in a week or so.

From: Kate
Sent: Monday, November 14, 2011, 4:43 AM
Subject: No Rush

Hi Tom:

Hope your Texas trip was great fun and that you're refreshed and ready to get back to work. I've recovered from my computer crash and have been making progress with the manuscript. The final chapters of the book are attached, five in all. It's a chunk and I understand that other things in your writing life come first, that you'll get to it as you are able. There's no rush.

My feelings about the quality of the writing and value of the story run hot and cold. Today I'm feeling positive. Tomorrow everything will look like brown drivel. I'm meeting with Elizabeth on Saturday to discuss next steps in the process of getting *Adrift* published, which is scary. I've lived with the story so long and hoped so hard that the risk of putting the book out and finding only indifference in the market seems too big a chance to take. There's comfort in a glowing screen at 4 AM because no one needs to know about this private obsession. As always, thanks for your help.

From: Tom
Sent: Monday, November 14, 2011, 4:15 PM
Subject: Feeling Like the Moon and the Stars

The only advice I can offer you is this: (1) Write the best book you can. Make sure it says things you really believe and are willing to stand up for. (2) Publish it. (3) Go write another.

First novels feel like the moon and the stars and all the world. But they are really just one step along a path that will include many novels and stories. We grew up with a quaint literary tradition, expressed in the movie *Finding Forrester,* that a great writer can produce one book that stuns the world and then everyone will wait years for his or her next opus.

Doesn't happen. Readers aren't looking for a wonder. They want someone who can do the magic for them, and if they love the work, they will look eagerly for another. So you want to get out there with your book and start working on the next one.

As to whether the world will love it or not, I'm often comforted by the line from C.S. Lewis's *The Screwtape Letters* paraphrased as, "a man is not usually called upon to have an opinion about his own talents, either positive or negative."

So do what you do to the best of your abilities and let others be the judge. I guarantee you that some people will hate your book, as some fraction of readers hate some of the books they try, and some people will love your book, as ditto they ditto. How big each fraction is will be a matter of the skill and heart you put into the work, plus some marketing and some luck.

Do your best. Move on.

From: Kate
Sent: Tuesday, November 15, 2011, 6:11 AM
Subject: Good Ol' Huntin' Dogs

Hi Tom:

Thanks for your words of encouragement—the reminder to do the work and stay balanced. It's duck season here on the Pacific Flyway and this year there's an unusually large number of waterfowl migrating to warmer climes. The hunters and their dogs are swarming the wetlands.

This morning I've been combing the Internet looking for sites that review books, studying ways to get my book onto sites, into book stores. I'm like an old hunting dog, jumping the gun, splashing in before the trigger is pulled. Thanks for hanging in there with me. Have a productive day.

From: Kate
Sent: Monday, November 21, 2011, 6:32 AM
Subject: Parties and Good News

Met with Elizabeth this weekend, attended an elegant book launch party in her honor, and sat down the next morning for a talk about printing and launching *Adrift*. Seems she doesn't have any plans to do more with her publishing imprint than publish her own books, doesn't want the distraction of managing other people's book projects.

She's too tactful and polite and lovely to say that directly, but it's the sense I got. And the prices she quoted for design were a bit beyond what I'd hope to pay. I was/am very disappointed. I'd hoped to pay a nominal sum, along with a small percentage of sale proceeds, to take the *Adrift* monkey off my back. Actually, I was looking forward to some help getting my book launched and welcomed the idea of working with Elizabeth in that way. She's so kind and supportive, a wonderful writing partner. Drove home Saturday half blind from a migraine headache and went to bed.

So, the good news. I got up Sunday at about 2 AM and went to work on Amazon's online CreateSpace for independent publishers. The attached book cover preview is the result. The cover photo is mine, taken of graffiti under Pike Place Market where Lizette would have been hanging out. I'm going to design my own cover and pay CreateSpace for the interior page design work. I downloaded their interior template and it looks like the learning curve to produce professional pages is pretty steep. I will learn what I can do with interior page design by working on some small projects that have been languishing. In the meantime, I'm going to publish *Adrift* through CreateSpace with their design help. So far it has cost me $49 for ISBN and premium distribution service. Elizabeth is right. It takes a lot of work to publish your own book and do a good job of getting it out there. I need to learn to do it myself, just like you and Elizabeth are doing.

Here goes. I'd appreciate feedback on the cover design, if you have a moment.

From: Tom
Sent: Tuesday, November 22, 2011, 9:17 AM
Subject: Diddling with Things

As to the cover graphic—which I tend to think of as Anxiety Girl—you're right, it will probably work very well in a cover thumbnail. And do tell the story in an "About the Cover," because it is so pertinent to your book's time and place.[1]

As to layering type over image on the cover, I've done that in PhotoShop with *Sunflowers* and *Trojan Horse* (which you can see on my Web site), because the cover photos (both from Getty Images) had appropriate blank spaces—and were partially chosen for that quality. With *The Judge's Daughter* the photo was too busy and formatted horizontally anyway, rather than vertically, so I put it between two strong color bands. Your cover image is in this category for lacking a blank space for title and author. Anytime you commission a work for cover, you have to instruct the artist or photographer to leave extra space above and below the subject for text.

As to the imprint, Media Group is a good choice. "Nutwoods" sounds a little, um, insane, but if you have a personal or family reason for choosing it and can explain it in a sound bite, if asked, then go ahead.

As to CreateSpace, I have no experience with any of the new publishing support groups. I can tell you—if I already haven't—that they will use your Word file as the basis of the text and probably not proof it. So you want your text stream (words, spelling and capitalization, bold and italic treatments, punctuation, interword spacing) as perfect as possible. But the page formatting (margins, type face and size, leading, headers, and treatment of chapter headings) won't matter to them so much.

Anyone doing page design will work in Adobe InDesign or FrameMaker or in some other popular page layout program and then copy your Word text into the appropriate windows. Any designer will have a basic model she or he has already worked up based on projected page size, then diddle with things like typeface and chapter headings. (For my ebook ePubs, I have a standard CSS and stick to it.) So, unless you make unique and difficult demands for the page look, someone experienced with the program could probably set the book up in a day's work. That doesn't mean to expect 24-hour turnaround. Contractors want extra time to allow for multiple projects, unexpected problems, etc. Could be a week or a month. (One more reason I stick to ebooks and learned to do things myself.)

Will you be selling paper books through Amazon? Will they actually take an inventory of books from a small, unknown imprint? It was the entire logistics of holding inventory and accepting returns (in a two-bedroom condo) that led me to leap on electronic publishing.

Notes:

1. Between this discussion and production on the book, the cover changed and no longer uses the graffiti image.

From: Kate
Sent: Tuesday, November 22, 2011, 7:10 PM
Subject: Going for a Spin

Hi Tom:

You are terrific! Yes, Amazon will carry both paper and eBooks on the Amazon Web site and they will take bulk orders from retail booksellers, although Amazon provides a 40 percent trade discount on books sold outside the Amazon system. So—Amazon gets 30 percent and the independent bookseller gets 40 and the printer gets 15. Not much left for the author. Amazon owns print-on-demand presses and doesn't job much out, so I've been reading. No inventory to warehouse and no return problems for the author. If consumer demand increases and a longer print run is required, the writer doesn't benefit from economies of scale and the lower per-copy price. The POD price is set and not negotiable, as I understand the contract.

Took a spin around my local Barnes & Noble today. Their Nook is front and center when you walk in the door, designer carrying cases, all sorts of doo-dads. Pricing: It seems trade paperbacks sell for between $12.99 and $15.99, so I'm thinking $13.99 would be the right price for *Adrift* in paper. $6.99 for the ebook. What do you think?

It's interesting when I look on the Amazon Web site that the price points between the two formats seem to be narrowing—ebooks for new releases are only a couple of dollars less than the paper version—the Steve Jobs biography, for example is $17.49 in hardcover, Kindle version is $14.49. I've been reading that Amazon has been wanting to up the price of ebooks once they get critical mass for a market and they're sure readers are hooked on the format. Looks like the time is arriving.

Since I'm a new author, don't want to price too high, but want to be able to cut the price if necessary and still retain some profit. I'm aware there are many free-for-download books and tons priced at $0.99, but Amazon doesn't pay royalties on anything priced below $2.99. They're gonna ask me about prices since it seems the author sets the price and then Amazon can decide to discount from there if they think it will sell more books. It's Amazon's site, but since the author sets the price, I'd prefer the author decides to do the price cutting. And the price for printing paper copies is fixed, so is the trade discount to book stores. So much for the complete control one enjoys by self-publishing.

We'll see what CreateSpace says about turn-around time. I told them I'd deliver the complete manuscript by Dec. 5, maybe get proofs in a week, take two weeks to turn the pages around. That would put the ball back in Amazon's court before I leave on Dec. 22 for Eau Claire WI to spend Christmas with my granddaughter and then to Boulder CO to spend New Year's with a long-time friend. I guess I could start selling books about Feb. 1. Don't worry, I don't think Amazon's site will crash from heavy traffic because *Adrift* is available.

So, that's it for now. I hope you and Irene have a great Thanksgiving. I'm going to cook up a storm because I like to and my sons enjoy it. Best wishes.

From: Tom
Sent: Wednesday, November 23, 2011, 9:40 AM
Subject: Pricing Theories

Kate—

As to Amazon paying no royalties for books priced below $2.99—that's not my understanding. Amazon and B&N have a two-level royalty system. For books above $2.99, they will pay authors 70% of list. For books below $2.99, the royalty drops to 35% because there are certain fixed costs of programming, server storage, and accounting and billing that they still have to pay. I think that's pretty fair. I don't think either of them distributes books for free, although sites like Gutenberg.com distribute out-of-copyright books for free.

Pat Larkin is watching my ebook progress closely, because he will soon be epublishing himself. I price at between $3.99 for the older books and $4.99 for the newer ones. He believes I would make much more by pricing at $0.99 and attracting more readers. The popular theory for $0.99 is that the price barrier to trying out a new author practically disappears when the price goes below a small Starbucks coffee.

I'm of the mind that once you drop that low, it's difficult to impossible to go back up. I currently hold to two theories on pricing. First, that the reader isn't just investing a dollar or four dollars or ten dollars in a book so much as mentally committing time to reading it. The reader isn't collecting scalps to display in a full Kindle library, but weighing the likelihood of wanting to immerse him- or herself in the world offered by the blurb and the cover art. (Anyway, that's part of my buying decision.) Second, in an entertainment market where two hours in a movie theater costs about $10, paying $5 for five or six hours of pleasure with a book is not such a bad deal. Besides, the prices I'm setting are where paperbacks were when I was first publishing, and it seems reasonable to keep these paperback replacements in that range.[1]

I have to rethink my definition of "print on demand." I'd always assumed this was a point-of-purchase thing: you walk into the bookstore of the future, decide you like the title displayed on the shelf, and the store runs a document center sort of operation in the back to print and perfect-bind your own copy. But what the son of a friend of ours is doing, and Elizabeth as well, is getting a tiny press run done at one time: 100, 500, or 1,000 books by laser print and perfect binding. This to my mind isn't so much "on-demand" as "Gutenberg writ small." I didn't want to mention this to Elizabeth when we met, but the publishing costs she was describing—on the order of $5 a copy, depending on quantity—are truly horrendous, compared to the per-copy costs in a large traditional press run. Between that and the wholesale price an outfit like Amazon will pay to stock the book, there's not much left for author or publisher on a competitively priced paperback.

I'm not sure about the prices between paper books and ebooks narrowing. The buyer still has to account for the cost of the ereading device and the relative inconvenience of having a book that can only be read on that device or its iPhone/iPad app. I tend to think the market's going to go the other way, although this is a projection for about ten years out, not this Christmas. Books you read for fun (mass market paperbacks, airport books, latest political insider) will go to electronic and low pricing. These kinds of books will virtually disappear in paper form because the costs of production and inventory will keep them from being profitable. Books you want to cherish and give as gifts (leather-bound *Lord of the Rings*, David McCullough's biographies, *Jonathan Livingston Seagull*) will stay in paper and their prices will rise, because people will still feel awkward about saying "Here, I got you a thoughtful gift card for buying Nook books."

As to your own pricing, the dollars sound a bit high to me—but you can float the book at those prices and drop back a couple of bucks if you don't get sales. Easier to go down than up.

I'll try to get you the last chapters today, so you're clear for the December 5 deadline.

Notes:

1. As of January 1, Thomas dropped the price of all his ebooks to $0.99. "Why let a few measly American dollars come between my readers and me?"

From: Kate
Sent: Wednesday, November 23, 2011, 12:13 PM
Subject: Buyer Behavior, Seller Beware

Hi Tom:

Thanks for the market analysis. I don't think it's too soon to start figuring out how *Adrift* might fit into the marketplace. And you are correct about the Amazon pricing structure—30% royalty for books below $2.99; 70% for those sold above that. I'll check the shipping costs, but I'm pretty sure authors get dinged for that, too. I thought the survey results

I sent yesterday on buying habits of those who use ereaders were interesting: More than 46% of those surveyed who say they acquire ebooks at least weekly (considered "Power Buyers" in this survey) report that they have increased their dollars spent for books in all formats, compared with 30% of all survey respondents who use ereaders. So, I guess that means Power Buyers are buying more in paper, as well as electronic formats.

The folks who conducted the survey say this statistic is important because Power Buyers have proven to be a bellwether of overall consumer behavior by three to six months. My guess is that as ebook prices creep up, power buyers and low-watt purchasers will become more discriminating. I have friends who love rummaging through the bargain basement of ebooks looking for a deal—a writer they like for an initially cheap price in the hope of finding more and better by the same author. They load up, against the day the dentist is running late or they've already seen the sitcom episode. Some of the 99-cent stuff is pretty rough. My friend Carol is a constant ereader. She told me the other day she was reading a bargain book on her Kindle and found this embedded in the text: "Cut. Too much description." I'm not sure she'll ever buy a book by that writer again.

Since I don't have an inventory of already published books I can't say what pricing strategy works best for the back list. I do think how older work is priced and presented is important in the strategic sense of supporting consumer interest in new work, which should carry a premium price compared to the old stuff. Guess I'll have to watch you and Pat. I do agree with the marketing wisdom that it's harder to go up in price than down. I'm not sure your pricing theories are right or wrong. I think those who fear boredom load up ereaders with impulse buys, along with the books of known quality that they save for later, like dessert. I don't think the click-and-spend set compares the price of a movie or the cost of an evening at the symphony. They just want a well-stocked cupboard and 99 cents is less than a can of soup.

You are correct again about the horrendous cost of print-on-demand. Elizabeth is pretty smart, however, and has probably figured out the angles. My understanding about how Amazon/CreateSpace works is that no matter how many sales, no matter how big the press run, if a book takes off,

Amazon always has the option of jobbing out the printing for a greatly reduced production cost. That is their decision and the author would not benefit in a share of those cost savings. The author would continue to pay the set POD price per copy. That is B.S. I'm talking through my hat here since I haven't published book one, but if *Adrift* were to sell in the 5,000 copy range I'd be looking for a traditional publisher. But, the royalty split is far less generous with traditional publishers. Amazon, they're getting a 30% royalty split and the cost of printing and shipping, which they probably get a big cost break on, too. It's a beggarly business, being a writer.

From my unscientific running around to bookstores and online booksellers, the price differential between paper and ebook appears to be about $3 to $4 for new releases. The differential may widen for older titles. I can only report what I'm seeing. If you see it differently, let me know. I'm trying to figure my ebook at about half the price of a paper book as fair trade from the author's perspective. I'm such a rookie, I may have it all wrong. I'm just trying to figure this stuff out and really appreciate going over it with you. Amazon may knock the price of my book down no matter what I think about price points and consumer purchasing theories and the most recent market reports and surveys.

I agree there will always be a place for paper books, but the market ratio: 70% paper vs. 30% ereader may get turned on its head in the future. I'm thinking in the 5-year range. I know I've got a lot of paper gathering dust at my house that I'd like to get rid of.

Just talked to Amazon's CreateSpace reps. They're ready to design the interior whenever I deliver the manuscript. If I focus and maintain my yoga practice schedule, I might make the Dec. 5 deadline I've set. Since I'll be traveling from Dec. 22 to Jan. 1, I'd like to get the project in the works, ball in their court. Really, I just want to get the *Adrift* monkey off my back so I can get on to other projects. I've obsessed about it long enough and I'm ready to let go.

Please don't hurry with the last chapters. The last thing I want to do is put pressure on you, believe me. I'm too respectful of your skill and time to do that. Finish when you finish. I'm fine. I think I'll go make some pumpkin pies. Take your time, please.

From: Tom
Sent: Wednesday, November 23, 2011, 1:52 PM
Subject: Nice Work

Kate—

Here's the end of the book. Very clean and a nice ending. Well, nice for Lizette and the people on Orcas Island, not so good for Sandy, Rocket, and the Dogs. I've made some simple edits and noted some word choices. The biggest issues you can handle easily with a sentence or a paragraph.

As to your market thoughts, yes, it's always been a beggarly business. But these are the best of times, right now, because you can get your work out in front of the public (along with 2 million other writers), where a couple of years ago you had to go through the gates of agents and editors who were looking for diamonds in mountains of sand.

My suspicion is that nothing's over yet, and things will keep changing and churning for a decade or more. My fear is that self-publishing authors will get comfortable with the 70% and 35% royalty rates offered by Kindle, Nook, and iBooks—and then the distributors, having gutted the traditional publishing world and hung it out to dry, will drop those nice royalties down to 10% and 15% and keep all the marbles for themselves. But then, if that happens, I still have my epubs—which are the universal electronic book format—and my Web site. I can sell books there and collect the money through PayPal. Readers can access them through simple software like Calibre (http://calibre-ebook.com/) and others that will come along. And if the government moves to control internet commerce, I'll think of something else.

It has always been a beggarly business, but my faith in readers abides. They're looking for quality, and when they find it, they'll recommend it. Despite all the marketing hype in the world, that's the way it's always been.

From: Kate
Sent: Thursday, November 24, 2011, 11:24 AM
Subject: Button Cloaks and Gratitude

Dear Tom:

I've gone over your wonderful corrections and suggestions and can't wait to get to work. I give thanks for you. And because you asked—the button cloaks or robes mentioned in the story are usually red and black, although I have seen green-and-black cloaks. They are sewn with mother-of-pearl buttons in traditional tribal design motifs and I've seen beautiful old cloaks at the Seattle Art Museum and anthropology museums at the universities of Washington and British Columbia. Didn't want to let the day slip by without expressing my gratitude. Hope your Thanksgiving Day is wonderful.

From: Kate
Sent: Sunday, December 11, 2011, 1:36 PM
Subject: Close But No Tiara

Hi Tom:

The results are in for the Mercer Street Fiction Prize and I feel like 2011 Miss Arkansas Alyse Eady, first runner up for Miss America—close, but no roses. The judge's comment is below. The manuscript was judged before 2/3 of your changes/corrections were made. With your help, I've polished long after the manuscript was submitted in October. I've entered *Adrift* in another contest, the Santa Fe Writers Project First-Novel Award. [The manuscript didn't make it into the finals.] And I may enter it in the PEN/Bellweather competition for an unpublished novel with environmental themes. I'm hoping for a good enough showing in these competitions to help create some buzz at publishing time this spring.

Finishing second in a competition with about 500 novel manuscripts [last count from the contest organizers] seems pretty good and it was easier with your sharp editing skills. I've learned a lot from you about putting a novel together and I'm very grateful to you for sharing your skills and talents. Thank you so much.

From: Tom
Sent: Sunday, December 11, 2011, 3:42 PM
Subject: Sorry You Didn't Win

Kate—

I am sorry you didn't take first. But take heart in that, fiction being such a personal thing, the choice among the top six must have been purely subjective and more influenced by familiarity and association with this story element or that, rather than with absolute writing or storytelling quality. Good luck with the Santa Fe and PEN competitions.

I'm down to the last three scenes, the finale after the denouement, of the time-travel book, which has the current title "The Children of Possibility." After that, I give it a day of rest and then do a read-through with fresh eyes. However, I don't expect too much rewriting at that stage—I've gone back and forth over the chapters as I work, and my internal sense is the story is pretty solid now. After that, I'll ask you, Pat, and a couple of others to give it a read-and-comment before I go to copyright and coding.

From: Kate
Sent: Sunday, December 11, 2011, 6:09 PM
Subject: Working at Warp Speed

Wow! It seems like you were just starting your novel when we met at Elizabeth's during Labor Day. I'm impressed. I guess practice provides quickness. I like the title of the book, but not the THE, just Children of Possibility. Can't wait to read it. I know it will be a great read.

I'm ready to submit the *Adrift* manuscript to CreateSpace. I'm going to wait until after New Years to submit. Don't know how long it takes to do the interior design and provide page proofs. I'm still noodling a cover. I sent the MS, CreateSpace cover, and some ideas to my friend in Boulder. I'll be spending New Years there and her daughter and grandson are both graphic designers. I'm hoping they'll surprise me with a cover design that's really special, better than what I came up with. We'll see.

And, if it wouldn't be an imposition, would you be willing to provide a blurb for the cover or the inside? I hate to ask you for a single thing more, but here I am again. I'd be honored if you'd say yes and will understand if I've overstepped the bounds of your generosity.

From: Tom
Sent: Monday, December 12, 2011, 1:29 PM
Subject: Update and Blurb

I think I was about halfway through the time-travel book by Labor Day, and the first 10,000 words were actually done about six years ago and left in limbo with a bunch of outline notes. But yes, I can work pretty fast now that I'm no longer doing the day job. I'll take removing the "The" from the title under consideration. It's actually an older language style that I find I've used throughout the book.

I note that you PhotoShopped the fangs out of the cover image you used on the Word Garden blog. That's probably a good idea, for the reasons stated earlier.

Here's a possible blurb. Let me know if you want me to tweak it in any direction.

ADRIFT Blurb – 121211

What do we owe to our past? What do we take into our future? Campbell uses the fragile persona of a young artist in the pivotal year 1973—after the music of the counterculture '60s has died, but before the steely patterns of the '70s and '80s became clear—to explore our human relationships with nature, family, creativity, personal responsibility, and love. Her characters are adrift, but one at least is moving steadily toward shore.

From: Kate
Sent: Tuesday, December 13, 2011, 6:24 AM
Subject: Feeding Gourmets

Good Morning, Tom. Your blurb is perfect, wouldn't change a thing. Thanks. Most reassuring to me, now and through the final edit of *Adrift,* is that you got/get what I'm trying to do with the story. I'm not confident that Mercer Street contest judge Rick Rofihe saw what I'm trying to do. Makes me worry that I've missed the mark.

There is the narrative through-line of Lizette's quest for stability and meaning in her life, which is fairly mundane thematically, but the story context is much larger than that. What I'm trying to illustrate are social/political policy decisions made in the context of the era that we're still grappling with today. I'm trying to quietly call for evaluation and understanding of the ramifications of those decisions in the context of now.

One of the women in my writer's group, who is working on a historical novel, described her book as "gourmet entertainment" for readers. I do not aspire to be a soft-shoe act, no matter how tasteful. Thanks, as always.

From: Tom
Sent: Tuesday, December 13, 2011, 10:02 AM
Subject: Do Your Job, Create a World

I have to admit that the direction of my blurb may have been influenced by things you've put into emails and said in conversation at Elizabeth's. However, I still feel the statement holds up in terms of what the book is and does. (I just don't get so many points for 20-20 insight.)

However, I'm not sure I'd push so far as to say that the book itself "illustrate[s] social/political policy decisions made in the context of the era that we're still grappling with today." Your use of news clips and the characters' occasional comments on them are more a motif of time and place, fixing the story in its setting.

But the real story is Lizette, maneuvering quietly and sometimes subconsciously through the wreckage of the lives around her, influenced by the good hearts of Marian, Abaya, and Poland. I don't think anyone reading your book is going to see it as an indictment of the Nixon years, price controls, OPEC, abandonment of the gold standard, Roe v. Wade, and all the other policy changes of the times.

This is not a bad thing, and it's not "a soft-shoe act." If you can make us believe that the character of Lizette is alive and has meaning, you have created a real thing that touches minds and hearts. To me, as a novelist, that is far more important that blazoning a set of political beliefs. The latter, as stories, are usually a disaster. For an extreme case, think of the Ayn Rand novels. Her characters are merely wind-up puppets mouthing her doctrines, or displaying their antithesis through the most comic acts of villainy. Political novels suffer in direct proportion to the amount of political belief they try to display. To tell a story that covers good ground and makes me believe in the characters is not "mundane." It's a success.

The troubling thought about your group member's description is the word "gourmet." She's trying to set herself above some level of mere entertainment. Well … first, get me to read beyond the first paragraph, and you have provisional clearance to present another ten or twenty pages. If I'm still turning them and not putting the book down in favor of something else, you're on track. If I get to the end and I'm amused, bemused, thoughtful, a little fascinated, and maybe disappointed that the experience is over (as opposed to going "… but … but … oh, shit"), then you've done your job. "Gourmet" comes extra, and it's for me as the reader to decide, not her or you as the writer.

Do your job. Create a world I can hold between two palms and actually believe it. That's hard enough.

From: Kate
Sent: Wednesday, December 14, 2011, 6:14 AM
Subject: Deflation

Thanks for your thoughtful remarks on the importance and role of story vs. polemic parading as art. You have a great knack for gently deflating my highfalutin' ideas—about art, self, and the world around me. Your advice about sticking to story in service to the reader is right on. I've debated about including a timeline at the end of the book that highlights the social/political context of the story and don't think it's worth more than two pages, if it's needed at all. I agree the story should speak for itself and not preach to the reader.

From: Tom
Sent: Wednesday, December 14, 2011, 10:03 AM
Subject: Going Wonky

Kate—

I don't see any problem with including the timeline at the end. In fact, as we discussed at Elizabeth's, a bit of back matter like this actually promotes discussion among reader groups, which is a good thing. (And I think it's preferable to the usual kinds of English 101 questions I see in group-targeted books: "What are Lizette's primary motivations? Have you ever felt that way yourself?") I've done a bit of copy editing—smart quotes, spacing, and stuff—on the timeline so that, hopefully, things won't go wonky if CreateSpace feeds your text into a mechanical converter.

The book still stands as a story.

T.

About the Authors

Thomas T. Thomas is a writer with a career spanning forty years in editing, technical writing, public relations, and popular fiction writing. Among his various careers, he has worked at a university press, a tradebook publisher, an engineering and construction company, a public utility, an oil refinery, a pharmaceutical company, and a supplier of biotechnology instruments and reagents. He published eight novels and collaborations in

Photo by
Robert L. Thomas

science fiction with Baen Books and is now working on more general and speculative fiction. When he's not working and writing, he may be out riding his motorcycle, practicing karate, or wargaming with friends. Catch up with him at http://www.thomastthomas.com/.

Books by Thomas T. Thomas
eBooks: *The Children of Possibility, The Judge's Daughter, Sunflowers, Trojan Horse*
Baen Books and eBooks: *The Doomsday Effect* (as by "Thomas Wren"), *First Citizen, ME: A Novel of Self-Discovery, Crygender*
Baen Books in Collaboration: *An Honorable Defense* (with David Drake), *The Mask of Loki* (with Roger Zelazny), *Flare* (with Roger Zelazny), *Mars Plus* (with Frederik Pohl)

Kate Campbell grew up in San Francisco, but has lived throughout California and the West. A working journalist, her environmental and political writing appears regularly in newspapers and magazines. Kate holds a degree in journalism from San Francisco State University and has studied creative writing at American River College and the University of California, Davis. She is a member of

Photo by Ching Lee

the Institute for Journalism and Natural Resources and the Squaw Valley Community of Writers. She lives in Sacramento and, in addition to writing fiction and poetry, publishes the Word Garden blog at http://kate-campbell.blogspot.com/.

12252564R00058

Made in the USA
Charleston, SC
22 April 2012